A Day with Marie Antoinette

A Day with Marie Antoinette

HÉLÈNE DELALEX

Flammarion

Archiduchesse Marie Antoinette, Sœur de l'Empereu[r] son Mariage avec Monseigneur Louis Auguste Dau[phin]

Contents

- 8 Foreword
- 12 The Icon
- 24 Princess and Dauphine
- 46 A Mother's Advice
- 48 "Queen of the Finest Kingdom in Europe"
- 55 "Your full-length portrait is my delight!"
- 68 Queen of Taste
- 88 Chinoiserie
- 92 Queen of the Trianon
- 111 The "Style Trianon"
- 112 Queen of Fashion
- 130 Extreme Coiffures
- 136 Queen of Beauty
- 149 The Queen's Diamonds
- 153 Queen of Pleasures
- 175 The Queen's Inner Circle
- 181 Queen of Hearts
- 191 "Elle"
- 194 Queen and Mother
- 205 "Chou d'Amour"
- 206 Queen of the Meadows
- 220 The Final Act

PAGE 1 *Marie Antoinette, Dauphine of France*, after Joseph Ducreux and Joseph Krantzinger, c. 1770.

PAGE 2 *Portrait of Marie Antoinette, Queen of France, in a Pannier Dress*, Élisabeth Louise Vigée Le Brun, c. 1785 (detail).

PAGES 4–5 *Arrival of the carriage procession bringing Archduchess Marie Antoinette to Versailles, 16 May 1770*, colored print.

FACING PAGE Detail from Johann George Weikert's painting *The Triumph of Love*, depicting the young Marie Antoinette dancing in this ballet-pantomime at the palace of Schönbrunn on 24 January 1765. This copy of one of the earliest known paintings of Marie Antoinette, painted in Vienna in 1765 by Martin van Meytens, was commissioned by the queen in 1778 to hang in the Petit Trianon. Marie Antoinette was particularly attached to this painting as it reminded her of her happy childhood.

THIS PAGE *Marie Antoinette, Archduchess of Austria, Queen of France and Navarre*, by Pierre-Alexander Tardieu, after François Dumont, engraving and etching, 1793–1815 (detail).

Foreword

She was fourteen when she arrived at the French court, too young to be capable of embodying the rigid constraints of court etiquette. At the end of her life, a prisoner in the Conciergerie, she was just thirty-eight but looked like an old woman. In the carefree insouciance of her teenage years, just as in the tragic unraveling of her reign as queen, Marie Antoinette was constantly out of touch and out of step with a world that was in decline, that she disliked and that disliked her, but that she would nevertheless defend to the end. These are some of the paradoxes of the life of a queen who was oblivious to the fault lines that were about to rend French society apart and that lend the figure of Marie Antoinette the romance and enigma that still surround her to this day.

This "average woman," according to Stefan Zweig, was destined to an extraordinay fate. To Chateaubriand, on his first meeting with her, she was "enchanted by life." A few years later, she was to be condemned to death as a "declared enemy of the French Nation." With time, such unequivocal judgments have softened: when Robert Hossein staged the play *Je m'appelais Marie-Antoinette* in 1993, he ended every performance by asking the audience to vote on the queen's fate. A majority voted to send her into exile. Dismissed by some as a fashion victim, admired by others as an icon of dignity, she may even be viewed as encapsulating both at once, a unique distillation of distinction and decadence. Caricature of capriciousness or merely a rebel, intriguing or immature, fêted at first for her grace before being accused of every species of perfidy, her figure continues to haunt our imagination.

With Hélène Delalex, heritage conservation manager in charge of the collections of the coach gallery at Versailles, we retrace the steps of a queen who has become a universal figure, so intimately associated with two brief decades at the palace of Versailles that she yearned to change even as it was disintegrating before her eyes. Here, her influence is everywhere. She inspired the flood not only of frivolousness but also of inventiveness that shaped eighteenth-century fashion—and that continues to inspire the shades of "puce," the panniers, and the brocades that feature in haute couture shows to this day. With her encouragement, her music master Gluck brought about a revolution in French opera. She influenced developments in theater, and herself performed at the Petit Trianon, where she and her architects contrived to reinvent court life. Her tastes steered marquetry towards new heights of refinement and nurtured a new vogue for lacquer ware. And her own story can be traced through the furniture that surrounded her: here the jewel chest for which she was castigated in the disastrous affair of the diamond necklace; there a little chair that she chose just before 1789, its original upholstery sporting a tricolor rosette added at the Revolution. Equally universal was the queen's defiance of convention and disdain for rules and regulations. She took delight in confounding expectations and in standing entrenched codes of behavior on their heads. She defined a style that flew in the face of what was expected of a queen, and that caused a sensation throughout Europe.

Hélène Delalex follows the breathless and unsettling pace of change set by Marie Antoinette at Versailles, visiting the sumptuous palace interiors that are imbued with her memory, such as the Gilded Cabinet or the Cabinet de la Méridienne, and the Queen's Hamlet, still so strongly marked by her presence and determination to break with the conventions of court life. Until that fateful day in October 1789, when she was forced to flee the palace of Versailles, which will always embody the ambivalences of her spirit.

CATHERINE PÉGARD
*President of the Public Establishment of the Château, Museum,
and National Estate of Versailles*

FACING PAGE *Marie Antoinette, Dauphine of France*, by Joseph Ducreux, c. 1770.

The Icon

Marie Antoinette. We need no other name to tell us who she was. In the popular imagination she remains the *last* queen of France; to the world in general she is *the* queen. No other woman was the subject of so many portraits in her lifetime; no other woman attracted so much attention in everything she did; no other woman embodied so many fantasies or inspired such extravagant adulation; no other woman in her time could more justifiably be viewed as personifying the cult of celebrity, in the modern meaning of the word. Still today she unleashes raw passions and arouses strong feelings, as though she were perpetually on trial: villainess or victim, ruthless Messalina or reckless romantic, frivolous queen or royal martyr?

Today she is an icon on a global scale. Sofia Coppola has made her a film star; books are devoted to her in ever increasing numbers; interior decoration magazines wax lyrical about the "Marie Antoinette style"; major fashion designers draw inspiration from her legacy; and her devotees view her as the embodiment of France, with websites, online forums, and associations forming a community of the faithful and selling merchandise of all kinds that multiplies her image to infinity.

PAGE 10 *T*he Queen's Staircase, built in 1680 and faced entirely in polychrome marble, leads up to the queen's state apartments at Versailles.
PAGE 11 Marie Antoinette wearing a redingote, unknown artist, c. 1780. According to tradition this sketch, which has clearly been folded several times, was sent by Axel von Fersen to his sister Sophie Piper as a model for one of the queen's gowns.
FACING PAGE Norma Shearer as Marie Antoinette in W.S. Van Dyke's eponymous film, 1938.

A GRADUAL RESURRECTION

Marie Antoinette's death was greeted by general indifference, and for some time afterward her fate was of interest to nobody. Then in 1815, a member of the house of Bourbon ascended the French throne once more and set about rehabilitating her image for the first time. Louis XVIII gave her the grandiose funeral ceremony that she had been denied, and commissions proliferated for history paintings depicting her as a martyr queen, her hands bound behind her and her dazzling white face gazing up to heaven. Marie Antoinette had lived the passion and death throes of the monarchy, and the monarchy was sanctified by her sacrifice. Among the faithful, a trade in her "relics" sprang up: a few words inscribed on a yellowing piece of paper, a handkerchief, a lace ribbon, a scrap of black stocking, or a slipper. Once the restored monarchy had fallen in its turn, the Empress Eugénie, one of the great beauties of her time, made a cult of her memory and started a collection of objects that had belonged to her. But despite all this, in the popular imagination, the world of sentimental Epinal prints, Marie Antoinette still remained only a shadowy presence in French history.

It was to be writers who would revive Marie Antoinette's fortunes. They saw in her a figure of fascination and tragedy on a suitably epic scale. While Alexandre Dumas made her the heroine of his novels, the Goncourt brothers, self-professed worshipers at the tragic queen's shrine, embarked on an impassioned quest to assemble every document pertaining to her life and scour every first-hand testimony. Their flamboyant literary style brought the most glittering years of her reign back to life, and painted her poignantly as a sacrificial victim. Their life of the executed queen was a triumph.

In the early years of the twentieth century, the shade of Marie Antoinette still haunted Versailles. During a visit in the summer of 1901, two English academics, Miss Anne Moberly and Miss Eleanor Jourdain, claimed to have encountered the dead queen in the gardens of the Petit Trianon, publishing their experience in a book that caused a sensation. A few years later, Pierre de Nolhac, the first director of Versailles, traced her footsteps through the abandoned palace and a deserted Petit Trianon, now overgrown and engulfed by nature. With every detail evoking the heady days of Marie Antoinette's reign, Nolhac created an impression that was akin, as the Goncourt brothers put it, to walking "through the toy box of a dead child." Captivated, he wrote magnificently on the subject of "his" queen. Finally, in the biography that he published in 1932 and that has remained in print ever since, Stefan Zweig painted a psychological portrait of masterly and unrivaled perceptiveness. Nowadays, throughout Europe and from Japan to America, Marie Antoinette has become a legend. Why should this be?

FACING PAGE *K*irsten Dunst as Marie Antoinette in the film by Sofia Coppola, 2006.
PAGES 16–17 Diane Kruger as Marie Antoinette in *Farewell, My Queen*, directed by Benoît Jacquot, 2011.

"*Her features and her demeanor reflected the very ideal of perfection in contemporary eyes. Slender, delicate, charming, gracious, playful, and coquettish, this nineteen-year-old girl became from the outset the goddess of the rococo, the epitome of fashion and of taste; any woman who wished to appear beautiful and attractive would model herself on Marie Antoinette.*"

STEFAN ZWEIG, *Marie Antoinette*, 1932.

FACING PAGE *Madonna as Marie Antoinette, performing "Vogue" at the MTV Music Awards, 1990.*

"THE MOST FEMININE OF ALL THE COURT LADIES"

First and foremost, Marie Antoinette was the dazzling reflection of her age. Her strong instincts and equally firm determination constantly to be at the cutting edge of fashion meant that she embraced all the passions that were most quintessentially of her time: its whimsy and lightness of touch, its gift for extravaganzas and theatricals, its worship of fashion and of nature, and the high regard it placed on the pleasures of friendship and intimacy. Marie Antoinette was also the original incarnation of the glamorous princess, "the most feminine of all the court ladies," according to the Goncourt brothers, the embodiment of youth and beauty, grace and elegance, forever dancing and pirouetting. Stefan Zweig, with his gift for the thumbnail portrait, observed that every woman knows the secret of her own beauty by some divine instinct, and this was why Marie Antoinette was perpetually in movement. It was in this shimmering, glittering vivacity that her true beauty lay. And it was because she was constantly in movement, mercurial and ever elusive, that it was so impossible—as she so often lamented to her mother—to "capture her likeness." At the same time, she also embodied the dying embers of the splendors of monarchy, the ultimate expression of that French talent for style and opulence that had proved so influential throughout Europe.

FACING PAGE *Portrait of Archduchess Maria Antonia of Austria*, attributed to Martin van Meytens, c. 1769. The young Austrian archduchess, aged thirteen in this portrait, already displays her distinctively candid expression and graceful carriage.

A MODERN PRINCESS

"She is imbued with the desire, or rather the absolute determination, to be completely independent," noted a secret report sent to Empress Maria Theresa in 1776. "She has let it be known at every opportunity, that she will not be governed, nor directed, nor even guided by anyone." While representing the last gasp of the Ancien Régime, Marie Antoinette was also the first modern princess, stubborn and wayward, with an independence and charisma that today recall Princess Diana. Representing a rejuvenated monarchy, breathing a hint of modernism into the rigidly unchanging world of the court at Versailles, she tried to free herself from the shackles and tyranny of her rank, challenging the rules and protocol that at Versailles had all the force of holy writ. As dauphine, she was candid and incapable of dissembling. She quickly dubbed the Comtesse de Noailles, her redoubtable lady-in-waiting, "Madame l'Etiquette," and took a mischievous delight in trying her patience with her whims and her refusal to toe her line. With her impish sense of humor, she was forever dissolving in giggles behind her fan, and no one was more acutely aware of the ridiculous absurdities of the old court. As queen, she refused to conform to the traditional role, remote and solemn, that she was expected to play, or to live a retiring life devoted to religion and charitable works: this was a queen who wanted to be not merely the king's wife, but also herself. Above all, this was a queen who for the first time aspired not only to "happiness," the new concept championed by Rousseau, but also—in her own words—to "the pleasures of a private life." But at the court of Versailles, where since the reign of Louis XIV the pageant and symbolism of the monarchy had been the mainstay of royal power, this was to have fateful repercussions that she could not have anticipated.

A TRAGIC DESTINY

Her death, finally, just before her thirty-eighth birthday, sealed her enduring fame. It is the brutal suddenness of her fate that strikes us today: the dizzying speed of her fall from the gilded salons of Versailles to the damp dungeons of the Conciergerie, and from the most magnificent throne in Europe to the scaffold. Caught up despite herself in a tragedy on a scale that was far wider in scale than her own fate, she would now emerge in her true light, and reveal capabilities beyond anything that even she could have imagined. It was only when she was losing her grip on the crown that Marie Antoinette began to show the strength and character of a sovereign queen. On the balcony at Versailles she was regal, facing the mob with calmness and courage; at the Temple prison she was majestic when—having learned from the clamor of the crowd that Louis XVI had been executed—she bowed to her son before giving way to her grief; and at her trial she conducted herself with queenly composure when, in the face of accusations of incest, she simply turned to the public galleries and said, "I appeal to all mothers here present." Her fortitude and dignity were such that even her opponents and her jailers were forced to admire her.

This is why she continues to move us today: this was a young woman endowed with many charms and graces, but in the end she was just a woman—at once strong and vulnerable, remote and human—with whom, ultimately, we can identify. The frivolous princess depicted by Sofia Coppola, the capricious teenager and whimsical slave to fashion, who plunged herself into a vortex of pleasures in order to escape her ennui, can show us something about the young people of today. The woman who rose above her sufferings has become a symbol of strength when all hope has gone, and courage against the odds. "It is in misfortune that we discover more of ourselves," as she herself recognized: but by that time it was already too late. ❧

RIGHT *Day of 16 October 1793*, Isidore Stanislas Helman after Charles Monnet, colored print, c. 1794–95.

Princess and Dauphine

Born November 2, 1755, Marie Antoinette was the fifteenth child of the Holy Roman Emperor Francis I and of Empress Maria Theresa, the last of the Habsburgs. The young Princess Maria Antonia spent a happy family childhood at the palace of Schönbrunn.

A CAREFREE CHILDHOOD

Etiquette at the Austrian court was relatively relaxed—especially when compared with Versailles—and the sixteen imperial children grew up in an atmosphere of considerable freedom. The young archduchess spent her time drawing, painting, playing the clavichord and pianoforte, learning to dance, frolicking with her little dogs, dressing up to stage little plays, having fun, and getting up to mischief with her many brothers and sisters. Delightful and vivacious, tending to laziness and mischief but good-natured, she was adept at charming her way out of the lessons her governesses set her.

FACING PAGE *Portrait of Marie Antoinette, Dauphine of France*, Austrian school, c. 1771.

MARRIAGE PLANS

After the death of the emperor in 1765, Maria Theresa reigned alone over the vast Austrian empire. In order to ensure peace in the empire and to strengthen the position of Austria, she systematically deployed her many children as pieces on the chessboard of European marriage alliances. From the moment of Marie Antoinette's birth, she had let it be known that she desired an alliance with France. In 1769, the diplomats of both countries bent to the task: in France the Duc de Choiseul, secretary of state for foreign affairs, persuaded Louis XV to accept this alliance, which would give physical expression to the rapprochement of the two most prestigious royal houses in Europe. Details of the marriage contract and questions of protocol were busily hammered out so that all would be in place for the following year, when Marie Antoinette would be thirteen.

It was at this point that Maria Theresa discovered to her horror just how sketchy her daughter's education had been, to the point where she could barely read and her spoken French left a great deal to be desired. The empress immediately dismissed her fondly indulgent old governess and replaced her with a teacher who would be much stricter. France offered its support in this venture by dispatching to Vienna the Abbé de Vermond, a doctor from the Sorbonne and librarian of the Collège des Quatre-Nations in Paris, with a brief to fill the gaps in the archduchess's education and bring it up to the required standard. In parallel, the dancer Noverre was dispatched from Paris to instruct her in deportment, and a dentist and hairdresser were also sent to polish up the future dauphine. But for the moment, it was a portrait of the future dauphine that was required.

Maria Theresa maintained stoutly that there was not a single painter in Vienna who was capable of capturing her daughter's looks. It was therefore a French pastellist, Joseph Ducreux, who was sent to Vienna for the purpose. On May 16, 1769, at the ceremony of the Lever at Versailles, Louis XV presented the resulting portrait to the dauphin in the presence of the assembled royal family, so revealing to him for the first time the features of his future wife.

On April 16, 1770, at the Hofburg Palace, the Marquis de Durfort, French ambassador to Vienna, transmitted the official marriage request to Empress Maria Theresa. As a token of the forthcoming marriage, a costly medallion containing a portrait of her future husband was pinned to Marie Antoinette's breast. The following day, in front of an assembly of ministers, the archduchess formally renounced the hereditary succession on both her father's and her mother's side. At five o'clock on the afternoon of April 19, 1770, the marriage was celebrated by proxy in the church of the Augustinian Friars in Vienna, with one of Marie Antoinette's brothers, Archduke Ferdinand, standing in for the bridegroom.

FACING PAGE *Marie Antoinette, Archduchess of Austria*, Jean-Étienne Liotard, 1762.

FACING PAGE This was the portrait, painted in Vienna by the French artist Joseph Ducreux in 1769, that was sent to France to introduce the features of the future queen to the court at Versailles. Conveying her graceful bearing, oval face, delicate features, ash blonde hair, soft blue eyes, and candid expression, this fine pastel portrait perfectly captures the beauty and charm of the young princess.

ABOVE This print of *Louis XV presenting the Portrait of Marie Antoinette to the Dauphin* by Jean-Baptiste André Gautier-Dagoty shows the Dauphin, the future Louis XVI, standing in the presence of the royal family and on the left of Louis XV, who is seated on the throne, as the portrait of Marie Antoinette by the French pastellist Joseph Ducreux (facing page) is unveiled to him.

ARRIVAL AT VERSAILLES

Two days later, Marie Antoinette set off in the early morning on the journey to her new country. Over two weeks later, on May 7, 1770, the procession of carriages reached Strasbourg, where her definitive crossing into her adoptive land was marked by the traditional ceremony of the "handover of the bride." On the Ile des Epis in the middle of the Rhine, in a wooden pavilion specially built to act as a "bridge" between Germany and France, the young archduchess was required to leave behind all her possessions and her entourage, and to renounce all links with the country of her birth. In a gesture of stark symbolism, she also had to take off all her clothes, before being arrayed in a magnificent French costume. Overcome by it all, she gave way to her feelings in the arms of her new lady-in-waiting, Mme de Noailles. But when she was addressed in German she collected herself and stopped the speaker short: "Do not speak in German, gentlemen: from today I will hear no other language but French."

Throughout the onward journey, Marie Antoinette was touched by the cheers of the people who crowded to watch her carriage pass; in June 1773 she remembered it in a letter to her mother: "What I found most touching was the affection and eagerness of those poor people, who despite all the taxes heaped upon them went into transports of joy when they saw me." On May 14, in the depths of the forest of Compiègne, Marie Antoinette at last met her husband in the presence of Louis XV, who offered her a warm welcome. Her meeting with the Dauphin was a rather stilted affair, by contrast, as the young man was pathologically shy and still very awkward in the company of ladies. Born on August 23, 1754, he was a mere fifteen years old, a year older than Marie Antoinette. On May 16, having bypassed Paris, the young couple made their entrance into Versailles.

The marriage celebrations that followed almost immediately were of unparalleled splendor, with the marriage blessing given in the chapel royal by the Archbishop of Reims, chaplain to the king. In the evening, celebrations continued at the royal opera, which had been completed for the occasion. The celebrations reached their climax three nights later in the most lavish and spectacular fireworks display ever given at Versailles, the result of two years of planning by the Menus-Plaisirs. The fireworks were followed by illuminations of the gardens, described as "the most magnificent ever seen at Versailles," with a network of connected wicks ensuring that sixteen thousand lanterns and lamps throughout the gardens were lit in under three minutes. With these flamboyant festivities costing over two million livres—"priceless," as the comptroller general of finances observed sardonically—Louis XV intended to demonstrate to the world that his kingdom was beyond any doubt one of the most brilliant in Europe. ଛ

FACING PAGE *Detail of the Royal Gate at the palace of Versailles.*

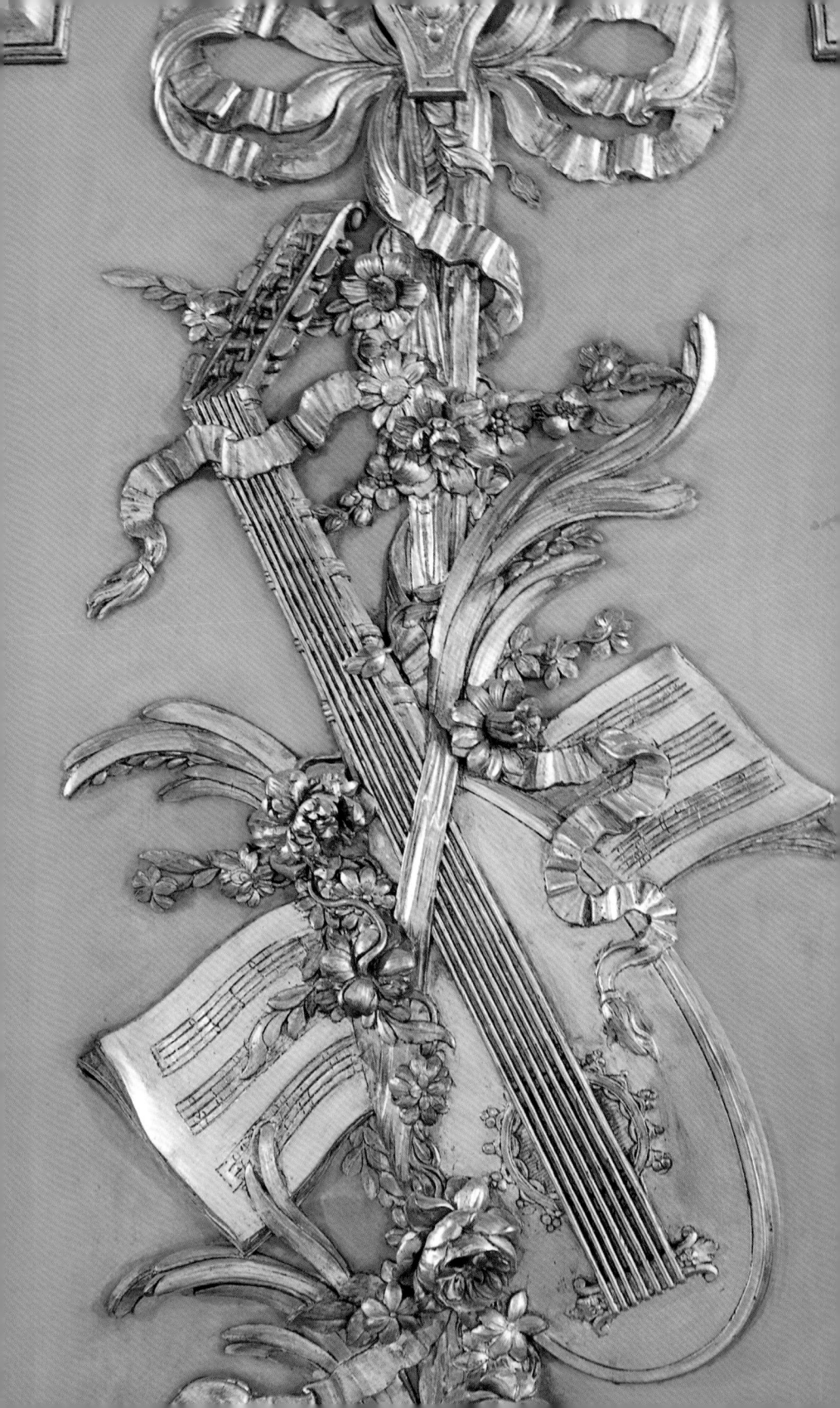

"*In the evening [on the day of the wedding]*, *all assembled in the well-appointed gallery. Most remarkable were the superb gilt busts bearing girandoles. The king appeared at half past six and started playing at a very large round table in the center. Everywhere the ladies gathered in groups, which, together with the remaining courtiers and some foreigners, filled the whole gallery with the most superb attire. The balustrade was left open for the ladies of Paris, who passed by one after the other and put on a splendid show on the other side.*"

DUC DE CROŸ, *Journal inédit*, 1770.

PAGE 32 Detail of the woodcarvings on the organ made by Robert Clicquot, organ-maker to the king, inaugurated by François Couperin in the Royal Chapel at Versailles at Easter 1711.

PAGE 33 The Royal Chapel at Versailles, built by Jules Hardouin-Mansart and completed by Robert de Cotte in 1710.

THIS PAGE AND FACING PAGE *The blessing of the marriage of the Dauphin and Archduchess Marie Antoinette of Austria in the Royal Chapel at Versailles, 16 May 1770*, colored print, Claude-Louis Desrais. This was not a marriage ceremony—which had already taken place by proxy in Vienna—but rather a blessing and renewal of vows.

PAGES 36-37 *Dress Ball for the Marriage of the Dauphin to Marie Antoinette, at the Versailles Opera, May 19, 1770*, drawing by Jean-Michel Moreau le Jeune.

"*Here you are where Providence has decreed you should live. In consideration of this great establishment alone, you are the most fortunate among your sisters and among all princesses.... Of the dauphin I may say nothing to you. You know how scrupulous I am on this point. A wife must submit to her husband in all things and have no concerns other than to please him and do his will. The only true happiness in this world is a happy marriage.*"

Letter from **MARIA THERESA** to Marie Antoinette, May 4, 1770.

PAGES 38-39 *Illuminations in celebration of the Marriage of Louis Auguste, Dauphin of France, and Archduchess Marie Antoinette, sister of the Emperor, May 16, 1770,* colored print published by J. Chéreau, 1790.
FACING PAGE Chart showing the princes and princesses present at the marriage of the Dauphin Louis and Archduchess Marie Antoinette at Versailles on May 16, 1770.
PAGES 42-43 *Fireworks display given by the city of Paris in 1785 in honor of Queen Marie Antoinette on Place Louis XV* (now Place de la Concorde), by Jean-Baptiste Philibert Moitte, gouache on paper.
PAGES 44-45 Detail of the layette chest of the Dauphin Louis Joseph, first son of Marie Antoinette, made on his birth on 22 October 1781, painted white taffeta. The lid is decorated with the monograms of Louis XVI and Marie Antoinette surmounted by cupids.

A Mother's Advice

When she left her home forever for Versailles, on the morning of April 21, 1770, Marie Antoinette took with her some reading matter that her mother made her promise to read on the 21st of each month, so that she would observe it faithfully. In these "Rules to read every month," followed by her "Particular instructions," the empress urged her daughter to pray every morning, examine her conscience, go to mass, and keep up a light diet of reading on spiritual matters, followed by a litany of practical advice: "be sure to participate fully in the customs of the court"; "never give rise to the slightest degree of scandal"; "never read any book without first seeking the advice of your confessor"; "pay no heed to others' recommendations, listen to nobody"; "do not be curious"; "answer everyone pleasantly, with grace and dignity"; "never do anything on your own initiative."

It is very clear that Maria Theresa was concerned that her daughter—whom she called a "scatterbrain" because of her flightiness as a child and her lack of discipline—might damage the reputation of Austria abroad. In the many letters that she wrote to her until her death—at times cheerful and affectionate, at others scolding and severe—she seemed to be forever looking over Marie Antoinette's shoulder, keeping an eye on her, giving her commonsense advice, reminding her in no uncertain terms of the way she was expected to conduct herself, and expecting her to account for her engagements and the company she kept. Maria Theresa sent off her first letter only a few days after her daughter's departure from Vienna, so that Marie Antoinette would find it waiting for her on her arrival at Versailles:

"Madame my dear daughter, here you are where Providence has decreed you should live. In consideration of this great establishment alone, you are the most fortunate among your sisters and among all princesses. You will find there an affectionate father who will also be your friend, if you should prove worthy. Place all your trust in him, you will be quite safe in doing so. Love him, obey him, try to divine his thoughts, you cannot do enough at this time, now that you are lost to me. It is this father, this friend who consoles me, who lifts me from my despondency and who is my only consolation, in the hope that you will follow my advice to cleave only to him, and to pay heed to all his commands and directions. Of the dauphin I may say nothing to you. You know how scrupulous I am on this point. A wife must submit to her husband in all things and have no concerns other than to please him and do his will. The only true happiness in this world is a happy marriage, and I know of what I speak. Everything depends on the wife, and whether she is willing, gentle, and amusing."

FACING PAGE *Emperor Francis I and Empress Maria Theresa with their Children*, by Martin van Meytens, 1754 (detail). Of the imperial couple's sixteen children—Marie Antoinette was the fifteenth—only ten would survive into adulthood.

"Queen of the Finest Kingdom in Europe"

On May 10, 1774, a throng of courtiers gathered to stare at the flickering flame of a candle in one of the palace windows at Versailles. At a quarter past three in the afternoon, the flame was snuffed out. *Le roi est mort! Vive le Roi!* "The king is dead! Long live the King!" The assembled company hurried to Marie Antoinette's apartments on the ground floor, where Mme de Noailles was the first to sweep a deep curtsey to the new queen of France.

FACING PAGE This first portrait of the young queen was painted in 1775 by Jean-Baptiste André Gautier-Dagoty. Marie Antoinette wears an astonishing court gown consisting of a low-cut boned stomacher descending to a point, and a billowing silk skirt over voluminously wide panniers. The skirt is embellished with ruffles of striped gauze, caught up with bows to which lilies are pinned, and over it all the queen wears a court cloak embroidered with fleurs-de-lis and lined with ermine. In the left foreground, the royal crown sits among lilies and roses on a cushion embroidered with fleurs-de-lis and trimmed with gold braid. Yet when this portrait was unveiled to the whole court in the Hall of Mirrors, it was immediately subjected to a barrage of criticism. So outraged were the assembled courtiers by the lack of resemblance to the queen that the portrait was decried as a crime of lèse-majesté. Her expression was found to be arrogant, moreover, as was the singular pose she had adopted, with one handed resting on a globe as though she intended it to be her dominion.

ADULATION FOR THE YOUNG QUEEN
Within days of her accession to the throne, Marie Antoinette wrote to her mother: "Although God has seen fit that I should be born into my present station, I cannot help admiring the work of Providence, which has chosen me, the last daughter among your children, for the finest kingdom in Europe." At Versailles, all eyes were on the young queen, and each of her appearances was greeted with greater wonder and envy than the last. In Paris, the people were positively infatuated with her, and she was genuinely touched in turn by the warmth of their cheers. When she made her entry into Paris the previous year, acknowledging the rapturous cheers of the crowd from the balcony of the Hôtel de Ville, the Duc de Brissac had murmured to her: "Madame, here are two hundred thousand people in love with you!" The eighteen-year-old queen, so full of grace, youth, and joie de vivre, represented the future of the kingdom. She was to usher in a new golden age for France, and the hopes and dreams of everyone in the kingdom were projected on to her.

"*The sculptor appears to have reserved all the art, precision, and smoothness of his chisel for the bust of the Queen, whom he depicts in her state robes. It is in marble, and Her Majesty wears a portrait of the king in a medallion. Her features combine grace and nobility to the very highest degree. This bust is far superior in this respect to the two portraits of our august sovereign that Madame Lebrun has successively offered to the public; and as it is this that chiefly characterizes her expression and bearing, the likeness is all the more perfect. The same grace and nobility shine from her coiffure, the details of which are captured with the utmost delicacy.*"

MME CAMPAN, *The Private Life of Marie Antoinette, Queen of France and Navarre,* 1822.

FACING PAGE *U*nveiled at the Salon of 1783, this marble bust is a tour de force by Félix Lecomte. The queen is depicted in all her splendor and majesty, but at the same time her expression is soft and human, and she wears a medallion of Louis XVI around her neck. The flowers in her hair and the lace trim and fabrics of her gown and wrap are rendered with virtuoso skill. The bust, now displayed in the Queen's Bedchamber at Versailles, belonged to the Abbé de Vermond, Marie Antoinette's Reader until 1789.

AN ILL-MATCHED COUPLE

The success of this alliance on the diplomatic stage was not matched by conjugal happiness in the private sphere. Rarely have two royal spouses shared so little in common in terms of their character and personality, their tastes and education, and even their physical appearance. Where Marie Antoinette was bubbling over with joie de vivre, Louis XVI was melancholy in temperament; where she was capricious, he was the embodiment of goodness; where she was passionate, he was ruled by reason and good sense; where she was full of mischief and rebellion, he was timid and prudent; where she was bold, he was modest; where she was sensitive and poetic, he was rough and ready; where she was winning and popular, he was solitary and wedded to the hunt; where she was extravagant, he was thrifty; where she adored parties and pleasure, he was engrossed by the sciences and manual work; and where she was graceful and desirable, he was rather coarse and unpolished.

For seven years the marriage remained unconsummated. It was true that both husband and wife were still very young, and that Marie Antoinette was put off by the idea of having children too early. Custom decreed that they should sleep in separate bedchambers, moreover, and at the slightest sign of a head cold Marie Antoinette would have no qualms in locking her door to the king—who in turn was so embarrassed by his physique that he was as anxious as she was to avoid this added chore. Soon whispers began to circulate at court about what was going on—or rather what was not going on—in the royal bed. And before long tongues were wagging throughout Paris society and gossip was rife about this frivolous queen and this impotent king who loved only the hunt.

Far from remaining a topic of discreet concern, the matter escalated into a veritable affair of state: without the birth of an heir, Marie Antoinette's very presence in France was compromised. The marriage contracts were scrutinized in order to determine whether the couple's lack of issue might lead to their annulment, international law was invoked, and there was speculation about the disgraced queen being sent back to her own country. Maria Theresa was alarmed to see the cornerstone of her entire diplomatic strategy being put at such immediate risk. As the months went by, her letters began to echo her worries, and she scolded her daughter for taking the matter too lightly, and offered her tips on caresses and embraces for the king. In April 1777, Marie Antoinette's brother Emperor Joseph II traveled to France in person in order to seek a solution to this singular diplomatic crisis. Having discussed the "item" openly with Louis XVI and listened to his awkward confidences, he advised him of the necessity of submitting to a "minor operation." On August 18, 1777 the marriage was consummated at last, and Marie Antoinette lost no time in writing to inform her mother of the great event.

ABOVE *Portrait of Louis-Auguste of France, Duc de Berry and Dauphin of France*, by Louis-Michel van Loo, 1769.

"Your full-length portrait is my delight!"

The time had come to create the official image of the new queen of France. In Vienna, Empress Maria Theresa already possessed eight or ten portraits of her daughter, but considered them all "perfectly dreadful, bearing no likeness whatever." She therefore urged Marie Antoinette to send her a "fine full-length portrait" from France, "for a room where the whole family is full-length." Proud of her lineage, the empress wanted to be able to show off to everyone the daughter who had made the best marriage of all her many children. As the months wore on she would brook no excuses, and became all the more insistent: "Since I have lost my darling little daughter and child," she wrote to Marie Antoinette on June 29, 1777, "my desire to know her as she has become must excuse my importunity, which springs from the depth and intensity of my maternal affections."

Marie Antoinette sat for one portrait after another, and was dismayed that none of the painters managed to capture the liveliness of her features and expressions: "Now it's my turn to be upset at not being able to find a painter who can capture my likeness: painters are the death and despair of me!" Her likeness was all the more difficult to capture because of her restlessness and impatience, and her reluctance to sit still. In July 1775, Jean-Baptiste André Gautier-Dagoty, a relatively unknown artist, completed the first official portrait of the queen. But when it was unveiled to the court in the Hall of Mirrors it came in for a barrage of criticism. In the face of this onslaught, Marie Antoinette decided not to send the portrait to Vienna after all. Subsequent portraits, whether in painting or sculpture, were equally heavily criticized.

It was in 1778 that the queen met the artist who was finally to provide the long-awaited portrait. Élisabeth Vigée Le Brun was beautiful, talented, and the same age as Marie Antoinette, and as the queen sat for her, so a friendship developed between the two. With her soft, smooth brushwork and the luminous whiteness of her pigments, she succeeded in capturing the nobility and youth of Marie Antoinette, as well as the dazzling complexion for which she was celebrated. Wearing no finery other than pearl bracelets, she is radiant. The portrait was a success. On April 1, 1779, after receiving this portrait for which she had waited so long, the empress wrote to her daughter, "Your full-length portrait is my delight!" The king's cabinet lost no time in having multiple copies made and circulating them throughout France.

PAGE 53 AND FACING PAGE *In* this large-scale portrait painted by Élisabeth Vigée Le Brun in 1778, Marie Antoinette is twenty-two and wears a magnificent white silk court gown with panniers. The royal crown sits on a cushion to the right, in front of a bouquet of flowers from which the queen has plucked a pink rose, which she holds in her hand. The artist here reinvented the genre of great court paintings by shedding their gravity and hieratic stiffness. Her treatment of the queen's heavy train embroidered with fleurs-de-lis, barely glimpsed behind her gown, is bold in its gauzy lightness.

THE QUEEN'S APARTMENTS

On becoming queen, Marie Antoinette left the dauphine's apartments on the ground floor at Versailles and moved into the queen's state apartments—the Grand Appartement de la Reine—on the first floor. Built in the reign of Louis XIV, the focus of these rooms was the Queen's Bedchamber. Every morning, as laid down by court etiquette, this was the scene of the ceremony of the Lever, at which Marie Antoinette received ladies of the court for private audiences. But what this room symbolized above all was the sole function of any French queen: that of bearing an heir to the crown. It was in this room that the nineteen royal infants born to the monarchs of the Ancien Régime were brought into the world, from the Grand Dauphin, son of Louis XIV and Maria Theresa of Spain, to Louis XVII in 1785.

While Louis XIV had conceived Versailles as a magnificent stage setting for the king, his successors abhorred the idea of being perpetually on view. Louis XV, and after him Louis XVI, fostered a private life away from court ceremonial, and within the palace laid out new private apartments for their exclusive use, more personal spaces designed for everyday and family life. Marie Antoinette's desire for privacy and freedom are clear to see in her extension of these private spaces, where only her intimate circle were allowed. As the state apartments were too grand and formal for her tastes, she had sumptuous private rooms laid out behind the alcove wall of the state bedchamber, as well as a suite of private rooms, the Petit Appartement; this opened directly on to the Marble Courtyard and was reached from the first floor by means of a concealed staircase, safe from prying eyes.

FACING PAGE *The* bed hanging in the Queen's Bedchamber within the palace of Versailles. Although its position has remained unchanged, the bedchamber was completely redecorated for Queen Maria Leszczynska—as may be seen in the magnificent paneling executed between 1730 and 1735 by Degoullons, Le Goupil, and Verberckt—and all the furniture was replaced for Marie Antoinette. On the morning of October 6, 1789, it was through one of the doors concealed behind the hangings flanking the bed, that Marie Antoinette fled, pursued by the mob, to seek refuge with the king. The alcove hanging, in white gros de Tours brocade embroidered with sprays of lilac, ribbons, and peacock feathers, was part of the summer furnishings, installed from spring to fall. The hangings in the apartments at Versailles were changed twice a year, in summer and winter. This is an exact facsimile, woven by Desfarges of Lyon, of the original hanging, also made by Desfarges in 1787.

IN THE BACKGROUND *Marie Antoinette flanked by the Three Graces and Clio, Muse of History*, design for the frontispiece for the catalog of the volumes in the library of the Dauphine Marie Antoinette, drawing by Charles-Dominique-Joseph Eisen, 1770.

PAGES 58–59 Brocaded lampas and silk hanging with appliqué medallions with silk embroidery and decorative arabesques, made for the billiard room in the queen's private apartments on the first floor of the Palace of Versailles by Jean Charton, 1779.

FACING PAGE, ABOVE, RIGHT, AND BELOW

Marie Antoinette's "diamond cabinet." This outstanding jewel cabinet, supplied for Marie Antoinette in 1787 by Jean-Ferdinand Schwerdfeger, was designed in the tradition of large seventeenth-century cabinets. Standing 8 ½ feet (2.63 m) high and 6 ½ feet (2 m) wide, and made of mahogany and mother-of-pearl with gilt bronze mounts by Thomire, it is one of the great masterpieces in the history of furniture making.

FACING PAGE AND LEFT

*T*he queen's private apartments were laid out on the ground floor of the place of Versailles in 1784. To reach them from her state apartments, Marie Antoinette would use the King's Passage. The walls of her bedchamber are covered with green taffeta; on one of the walls hangs Louis Auguste Brun's portrait of Marie Antoinette on horseback, while on the commode, embellished with gilt-bronze mounts, stands a terracotta bust of Louis-Antoine d'Artois, Duc d'Angoulême, son of the Comte d'Artois, brother of Louis XVI and future Charles X.

ABOVE *Marie Antoinette, Queen of France*, Louis Cournerie, miniature on ivory, c. 1840–70.
FACING PAGE Although Marie Antoinette had little taste for reading, she nevertheless needed to have a library that befitted her rank as queen. The two libraries created for her in her private apartments in 1772, when she was still dauphine, were refurbished seven years later. Her former tutor, the Abbé de Vermond, remained her Reader until July 1789. Above all, these rooms represented for Marie Antoinette a place where she could snatch moments of peace and solitude, surrounded by her books. The bookcases hold Marie Antoinette's books, bound in calfskin or morocco leather and stamped with the royal arms. The library doors are decorated with faux bindings, the bookcase doors conceal rack and pinion shelves for consulting the works, and the drawer handles are in the shape of the imperial eagle.

FACING PAGE The Cabinet de la Méridienne was the most intimate room in the queen's apartments. In 1781, to mark the birth of the dauphin, Marie Antoinette commissioned her architect Richard Mique to redecorate this octagonal boudoir. The angled doors allowed servants to pass from the queen's bedchamber to the library without disturbing Marie Antoinette. Placed in a mirrored alcove is the sofa (*méridienne*) on which the queen would rest during the day, and which gave the boudoir its name. The alcove also contains a remarkable gueridon with a top of petrified wood, made in Vienna in 1770 by Anton Matthias Domanöck, a gift to Marie Antoinette from her mother Maria Theresa on her definitive departure from Vienna for Versailles.

BELOW Detail of the armchair à la reine in carved and gilded walnut made for the Cabinet de la Méridienne around 1785 by Georges Jacob. The armrests feature sphinxes and lapdogs, while the uprights of the backrest consist of fasces crowned with flames.

Queen of Taste

In matters of decoration and furnishings—unlike in the fine arts—Marie Antoinette displayed firm instincts, well-defined tastes, and striking consistency. For her private rooms, the queen—always avid for the latest fashions—commissioned innumerable new makeovers, unrestrained by any considerations of time or budget.

BELOW *D*etail of the decorative woodwork in the Cabinet de la Méridienne. The elaborate carvings by the Rousseau brothers celebrate the royal couple's conjugal love and the birth of the dauphin.
FACING PAGE *Marie Antoinette with a Book*, by Élisabeth Vigée Le Brun, 1778.

NEW DECORS IN THE LATEST FASHIONS

While her bedchamber retained its handsome decorations from the reign of Louis XV, the queen chose all the latest fashions for her private apartments, her restless hunger for new ideas bringing about ever more rapid changes. In 1779, wanting to refresh the decorations in her private Grand Cabinet, she commissioned an "extraordinary" rich white silk satin brocade, patterned with floral arabesques and medallions, for the curtains, portieres, wall hangings, seats and bed hangings, fire screen, and room screen. This tour de force of the Lyon silk industry, displaying astonishing finesse and craftsmanship and costing over 100,000 livres, was nonetheless removed less than four years later, when Marie Antoinette decided instead to panel the room throughout.

The Rousseau brothers, decorative sculptors, created paneling in the arabesque style of great elegance and finesse. Their work, combining virtuoso skills with a restraint that befitted the classicism of Versailles, was a feature of Marie Antoinette's finest interiors. The excellence of the paneling in the Gilded Cabinet and the Cabinet de la Méridienne is an example of the pinnacle of late eighteenth-century decorative art.

"*My tastes are not the same as those of the King, who is interested only in hunting and mechanical contraptions. You must admit that I would cut a curious figure at a forge; I should be no Vulcan, and the part of Venus might displease him more than my tastes of which he disapproves.*"

Letter from **MARIE ANTOINETTE** to Comte François de Rosenberg, April 17, 1775.

PAGES 70-71 *The* Boudoir de la Reine or silver bedroom at Fontainebleau, 1786. The silver background to the painted decorations on the walls (in fact painted in white gold) by Michel Hubert Bourgeois and Jacques Louis François Touzé and the outstanding mother-of-pearl veneered furniture by Riesener (see page 81) together form a peerless example of the refinement and harmony of the decorative arts on the eve of the Revolution.

FACING PAGE Design for the embroidery for the counterpane for the Queen's Bedchamber at Versailles, workshop of Marie-Olivier Desfarges (detail), gouache, 1786.

ABOVE AND FACING PAGE *C*reated in 1777 to plans by the architect Richard Mique, the astonishing Turkish Boudoir at Fontainebleau was a gift from Louis XVI to his wife, whose bedchamber had no boudoir. The decoration consisting of turbans, cassolettes, perfume-burners, strings of pearls, crescent moons, and ears of corn, bears witness to the vogue for exoticism.

ABOVE *Perfume* burner bought by Marie Antoinette at the sale of the Duc d'Aumont's collection in 1782. The exquisite bowl in red flower jasper rests on a richly decorated tripod base in chased and gilt bronze; engraving after Pierre Gouthière, from the catalog *Le Cabinet du duc d'Aumont et les amateurs de son temps*, Aubry, Paris, 1870.

FACING PAGE The Gilded Cabinet was the principal room in the queen's private apartments at Versailles. In the afternoon she would grant private audiences there, give musical recitals or pose for Élisabeth Vigée Le Brun. The paneling, carved by the Rousseau brothers in 1783 under the direction of Mique, is a veritable tour de force: executed with virtuoso finesse, it is an outstanding example of the classical revival style that followed the excavation of Pompeii and Herculaneum. The large sphinxes, meanwhile, bear witness to early signs of the vogue for the Etruscan style and the passion for all things Egyptian in the 1780s.

PAGES 78-79 In 1770, the young dauphine Marie Antoinette received this exquisite jewel casket by Martin Carlin as a wedding present. Embellished with marquetry in rosewood, sycamore, yew, and ebony, enriched with chased and gilt bronze mounts and inset with Sèvres porcelain plaques, the piece was designed as a writing table—the drawer opens to reveal a velvet-covered writing surface and writing case—topped by a casket designed to hold the queen's jewel cases. This new and sophisticated item of ladies' furniture was soon the latest fashion, with Madame du Barry, as well as Marie Antoinette's sisters-in-law, the Comtesse de Provence and the Comtesse d'Artois, commissioning one for their own use.

FURNITURE OF REFINEMENT

Throughout her reign, Marie Antoinette issued ever-increasing numbers of commissions for furniture and objets d'art: *meubles meublant*, or static pieces arranged against a room's paneling, of which it was an extension; and *meubles volant*, or movable pieces which could easily be moved to a different position in the room. The latter category included armchairs upholstered in rich fabrics; marquetry commodes in precious woods including rosewood, violet wood, amaranth, citron wood, sycamore, tulipwood, maple, and mahogany; and console tables embellished with bronze mounts and inlaid with tortoiseshell, mother-of-pearl, copper, and porcelain. Marie Antoinette prized above all the work of the German-born cabinetmaker Jean-Henri Riesener, who injected fresh inspiration into the aesthetics of French furniture. The queen passed these commissions via the department of the Garde-Meuble de la Couronne as well as through her own Garde-Meuble, an establishment that she contrived to make autonomous and to endow with substantial funding.

BELOW *The Boudoir of Marie Antoinette*, Jules Marc Antoine Frappaz, 1876.

FACING PAGE Detail of the cylinder desk embellished with lozenge-shaped mother-of-pearl inlays set in a latticework of gilt copper, with satinwood, box and ebony veneer, supplied c. 1786 by Jean-Henri Riesener for Marie Antoinette's boudoir at Fontainebleau.

PAGES 82–83 Detail of the commode supplied in 1782 by Jean-Henri Riesener for the queen's bedchamber at Marly, now in Marie Antoinette's Gilded Cabinet. The front is covered with exquisite trellis marquetry lozenge and fleuron mosaic set in amaranth, while the trapezoidal central door bears a marquetry panel of agricultural implements set in a large medallion. The waist, front, corners, and feet are richly decorated with garlands and flowers in chased and gilt bronze.

EXQUISITE DINNER SERVICES
While Louis XIV subjected himself daily to the public ritual of the "Grand Couvert," Louis XVI and Marie Antoinette observed this tradition of dining in front of the court only on Sundays and feast days. Once their audience had taken their places and the first dishes had been arranged on the table, the king and queen would make their entrance. In a service *à la française*, which first appeared in the seventeenth century, the meal was divided into several courses, with over forty dishes presented simultaneously and arranged symmetrically on the table. The king and queen could then choose from the great variety of dishes. Each new course appeared like a perfectly choreographed ballet, with a procession of officers of the service known as La Bouche ("The Mouth") carrying in the dishes and placing them on the table. After 1820, this type of service was replaced by service *à la russe* or *à l'anglaise*, in which dishes were brought in successively, as they are today.

If Marie Antoinette preferred more intimate suppers, it was the opulence of her dinner services that made the most impression during her reign. Her gold, silver, and porcelain services were of exquisite refinement, as may be seen in the Sèvres dinner service with a "border rich in colors and gilding," the most costly to be supplied to the queen. This tour de force comprised over 300 pieces, including soup plates and dinner plates, terrines and dishes, sauce boats, butter dishes, mustard pots, eggcups, large oval platters, fruit bowls, ice cups, and ice buckets for cooling glasses and bottles. On June 22, 1784, during a royal visit to France, Louis XVI presented this remarkable service to the Swedish king Gustav III. A second identical service was immediately commissioned for Marie Antoinette and delivered on August 26 of that year.

ABOVE Soft porcelain *pot à jus* from the service "rich in colors and gilding" supplied by the royal porcelain factory at Sèvres in 1784, and bearing the date letter "G" for this year.
FACING PAGE Plates made at the Sèvres royal porcelain factory. Center, top: soup plate from the service "rich in colors and gilding" supplied to the queen in 1784; the plate is decorated with a central medallion containing a bouquet of roses inside a pearl border against a blue ground, with oval cartouches edged in blue or red and containing pansies on the borders, linked by a frieze of roses and cornflowers painted on a wine-colored ground. The whole design is bordered with pearls and laurel garlands and embellished with extremely rich gilding. Center, bottom: dinner plate from the "pearl and cornflower" service supplied in 1782 for the Petit Trianon. The design of this 293-piece service features bouquets and friezes of cornflowers, with strings of pearls on a green ground.

THE "MARIE ANTOINETTE STYLE"

The "Marie Antoinette style" might be defined as a taste for spaces flooded with light, a palette dominated by white, and a classical style of airy lightness and delicacy, with a decorative repertoire featuring flowers, pearls, and medallions. It was also characterized by a fondness for furniture embellished with bronze mounts in the form of faux draperies, fringes, ruffles, and ribbons. Above all, it rested on the illusion of simplicity, when in reality every element bore witness to skills and arts of formal perfection and peerless refinement. The perfect harmony between the mural decorations, gilding, colors, forms, furniture, and objets d'art, with the various decorative arts echoing and balancing each other, created a "harmony of ensembles," as Pierre Verlet called it: a setting of splendor and perfection that would forever be associated with French style.

BELOW The paneling in the Salon de Compagnie at the Petit Trianon, intricately carved by Honoré Guibert, is embellished with musical trophies above, and the monogram of Louis XV below, with the two "L"s in myrtle leaves intertwined with three lily flowers and crowned with a wreath of roses.

FACING PAGE The Salon de Compagnie, on the piano nobile, was devoted to games, music and conversation. The impressive fireplace is in violet breccia marble; the "damask in three colors," predominantly cherry red, has been re-created by the silk-weavers of Lyon.

Chinoiserie

In the mid-eighteenth century, France was gripped by a passion for all things Chinese. Ever since Jesuit missionaries in the reign of Louis XIV had first revealed the mysteries of the Orient, French enthusiasm for this immense and fabled empire had never ceased to grow. While the thinkers of the Enlightenment praised the humanist philosophy of Confucius and an ideal model of government, in Paris and at court people were fascinated by the objets d'art, fabulous silks, lacquer screens, and peerless porcelain that were being imported by the French East India Company.

During her childhood at Schönbrunn, Marie Antoinette had developed a taste for Oriental art through the lacquer and porcelain collections of her mother, Empress Maria Theresa. When she became queen, she swelled her collection of Japanese lacquer boxes, already one of the largest in Europe, with numerous purchases from *marchand-merciers*; collected Oriental porcelain, which she enriched with lavish bronze mounts in the latest fashion; and commissioned new Sèvres services decorated "in the Chinese style." This new decorative repertoire, echoed on silks, wallpapers, bibelots, and fans, was composed of charming motifs and fantasies reflecting an Orient of the imagination, an exotic mélange of mandarins with trailing mustaches and formal robes embroidered with dragons, jade pavilions with upturned roofs, whimsical mountain scenes, parasols decorated with flowers, pagodas, little wooden bridges, mythical dragons, acrobatic monkeys, and birds of a thousand hues.

FACING PAGE *T*he Chinese pieces imported by the French East India Company inspired models manufactured by the royal porcelain factory at Sèvres, such as this large "egg" vase, the central piece of a garniture of three vases supplied in 1775–76 for the queen's private apartments at Versailles. The porcelain vases with Chinese-style decoration are richly embellished with chased and gilt bronze mounts attributed to Jean-Claude-Thomas Chambellan-Duplessis. The painted decoration by Louis-François Lécot makes lavish use of gilding, both in the exquisite garden with its exotic plants and in the slender fillets outlining the figures.

FACING PAGE *T*his three-tier box on console legs was part of Marie Antoinette's collection of Japanese lacquer, most of which was bequeathed to her by her mother in 1780. This collection of seventy boxes of huge variety and imagination was displayed in her Gilded Cabinet, arranged on four tables and in a vitrine embellished with outstanding Japanese black lacquer panels, known as the "lacquer cages", supplied by Jean-Henri Riesener in 1783. The decorative motifs on this box play on the contrasts between the stippled lacquer and naturalistic motifs of birds and flowers, and the strictly geometric black-and-gold striped sections.

ABOVE The most spectacular lacquer pieces were displayed on tables with petrified wood tops, including this lacquer box in the form of a little spotted dog lying on a low pedestal.

Queen of the Trianon

"Madame, you love flowers. I have a bouquet to offer you. It is the Petit Trianon." On May 24, 1774, Louis XVI presented Marie Antoinette with a passe-partout key set with 531 diamonds, created by Maillard, jeweler to the Menus-Plaisirs. With this symbolic gesture, Marie Antoinette became queen of her new realm, the Petit Trianon.

THE "PETIT CHÂTEAU DE TRIANON"

Less than ten years after it was built, at the instigation of Mme de Pompadour during the reign of Louis XV in order to "relieve the king's boredom," the Petit Trianon became the exclusive domain of Marie Antoinette. Still today, for the thousands of visitors who flock here from all over the world, it embodies the private face of Versailles, and the pleasures of a queen who—contrary to all established custom—here gave orders in her own name.

Inside, Marie Antoinette was content with the Louis XV decorations, especially on the piano nobile where she spent most of her time, in the reception rooms and the three smaller mezzanine rooms that made up her apartments. On the walls she hung paintings that reminded her of her family and her childhood in Vienna, prompting people to call it her "petit Schönbrunn." The only major works she carried out there were in 1776, when the famous Cabinet of Moving Mirrors was created. This remarkable boudoir, next door to her bedchamber, was lined with mirror panels that could be raised from basement level by an ingenious mechanism, so screening the windows and insulating the room completely from the outside world. At night, viewed by the infinite reflections of candle flames, the room seemed to take on infinite proportions.

FACING PAGE View of the Petit Trianon from the first-floor landing at the top of the main stair. In the background is the small stair leading to the attic story.

"*Rooms that were undoubtedly exceedingly elegant in their furnishings and decorations, but in no case very lavish: pure good taste in place of the expected luxury.*"

PIERRE DE NOLHAC, *La Reine Marie Antoinette*, 1890.

FACING PAGE The Cabinet of Moving Mirrors in the Petit Trianon. In 1776, the queen commanded Mercklein and Courbin, mechanic and locksmith to the court, to create a novel system of mirrors that could be raised and lowered by means of pulleys, so transforming the room's windows into mirrors and isolating it from the outside world. In 1787, Marie Antoinette commissioned new paneling: this elegant pale blue and white paneling, intricately carved by the Rousseau brothers to designs by Mique, is among the most exquisite at Versailles.

PAGES 96–97 *View of the Petit Trianon and the Temple of Love*, watercolor by Louis Nicolas de Lespinasse, from *Le Voyage pittoresque de France*, Paris, 1780.

THE QUEEN'S "PRIVATE EXCURSIONS"

"Now she had her new toy, one of the most exquisite confections of French taste that ever existed", wrote Stefan Zweig. Never was Marie Antoinette happier at Versailles than during the time she spent at the Petit Trianon, especially in summer, when her stays there became ever more prolonged. In this enchanted realm, her new haven of privacy and intimacy, she liked to say that she lived like a "private person," and that when she was there she was no longer the queen but simply herself. In this small chateau designed for intimacy there was no pomp or ostentation. Eager to show herself as an attentive hostess, she took with her only a few female servants from her retinue, and entertained in a relatively simple style. Among her inner circle there were her sister-in-law Madame Élisabeth, her close friends, and soon her children. The king was a frequent visitor, but was allowed there only at her express invitation. And although an apartment was reserved for him in the attic storey, he always returned to the palace to sleep.

At the Petit Trianon, court etiquette was relaxed: Marie Antoinette insisted, for example, that when she entered a room no one should curtsey or bow to her. She also banished the court dress code, as Mme Campan noted: "A white percale gown with a gauze fichu and straw hat was the sole adornment of princesses." Afternoons were spent strolling along the riverbanks, delighting in the sounds of waterfalls and scents of flowers in bloom, or conversing in the salon, the ladies stitching their tapestry work or playing the pianoforte and the gentlemen playing cards or backgammon, before taking supper and going back to Versailles. "The Trianon was a world in miniature," observed Stefan Zweig. "From its windows—symbolically—one could see nothing of the town, of Paris, of the countryside, or of anything connected with real life. So modest were its grounds that it would take only a few minutes to cross them, yet this tiny space was of more significance to Marie Antoinette and meant more to her than the whole of France and her twenty million subjects."

PAGES 98–99 View of the Temple of Love, in the gardens of the Petit Trianon. "I know of nothing more beautiful than this temple," wrote the Prince de Ligne, "It is the acme of perfection and taste." Standing on a small island reached across two little bridges lined with jardinières, the Temple of Love formed one of the most celebrated vistas at the Trianon. Built by Mique in 1778 to designs by Hubert Robert. Twelve alabaster columns support a cupola decorated with symbols of love, including wreaths of roses, quivers, and arrows linked by ribbons and olive branches. In the center is a statue by Bouchardon of Cupid cutting his Bow from the Club of Hercules, completed in 1746. Marie Antoinette was enchanted with this confection, which she could admire from the windows of her bedchamber.

BELOW Hyacinth "Marie-Antoinette," from *Le jardin Eden ou le paradis terrestre renouvellé dans le jardin de la Reine à Trianon*, Pierre Joseph Buc'hoz, 1783–85. Among all the flowers at the Trianon, the queen had a special fondness for hyacinths. In 1784, she ordered 354 hyacinth bulbs in a variety of colors, followed by over a thousand more in 1778, three hundred of which were to decorate her bedchamber in the winter months.

FACING PAGE In this charming portrait painted by Antoine Vestier in around 1780, the young queen poses proudly in front of the Temple of Love and her new gardens at Trianon; in her right hand she holds a cane and in her left hand a glove, while her large straw hat decorated with feathers is cast nonchalantly to one side.

GARDENS OF ENCHANTMENT

It was above all the fairytale setting provided by its gardens that made the Petit Trianon the queen's favorite spot. Marie Antoinette had a vision of the Petit Trianon as a bucolic idyll, an eighteenth-century Arcadia, the reflection of a vanished golden age. One of the first things she decided to do after taking possession of her new domain was to abolish Louis XV's famed botanical garden, a "plantsman's and scholar's garden" planted by the gardener Richard and the botanist Bernard de Jussieu, a botanical treasure store celebrated throughout Europe and brimming with rare and exotic plants. She gave all the plants to Buffon, who had them taken to Paris.

In conforming to the vogue for gardens that were *au naturel*, Marie Antoinette was not only following the latest fashions in gardening, but she was also giving expression to a new sensibility widely explored in the literature of the second half of the eighteenth century, and most notably by Rousseau in his novel *Julie, or the New Héloïse*, published in 1761 and in numerous editions thereafter: "What is the meaning of these paths, so straight and sandy, that are to be found everywhere; or of these star-shaped intersections that, far from making gardens look large to the eye, as we imagine, only serve to draw clumsy attention to their limitations?... Is nature forever busying herself with set square and ruler?" The garden à l'anglaise, in contrast to the traditional French model as developed by Le Nôtre, reflected new social aspirations, a different way of living, the promise of a new freedom. Above all, with its meandering paths with no visible goal, it was the ideal place for strolling and daydreaming.

Work began in 1774, and by 1782 the garden was finished. In this pastoral idyll according to the imagination of Richard Mique, first architect to the king, the land was completely reshaped, and the garden—with its sinuous paths, gentle valleys, and serpentine streams, its miniature mountains and picturesque viewpoints, its romantic grotto and rustic waterfalls, its rocks and ravines, its follies, bridges, and classical temples—was changed beyond recognition. "I thought I had gone mad or was dreaming when I found, instead of the largest hothouse in Europe, high mountains, a great rock, and a river! Never have two acres of land changed so much in shape, nor cost so much money!" exclaimed the Duc de Croÿ, who had not clapped eyes on the Petit Trianon since the death of Louis XV. In the end, this new art in the guise of nature, shaped by the gardener's invisible hand, was every bit as ruinously expensive as the most ambitious of Le Nôtre's formal designs.

FACING PAGE *Recueil des plans du Petit Trianon, par le Sr Mique, Chevalier de l'Ordre de St. Michel, Premier architecte honoraire, Intendant Général des Bâtiments du Roy et de la Reine*, Claude-Louis Châtelet, 1786. These albums painted in gouache were given by Marie Antoinette to the select guests for whom she threw lavish celebrations at the Trianon.

PAGE 104 Élisabeth Vigée Le Brun's *Portrait of Marie Antoinette in a Chemise Dress* caused a scandal at the Salon du Louvre of 1783.

PAGE 105 The Belvedere, built by Richard Mique in 1777, was used by Marie Antoinette as a music room. The octagonal building has a mosaic floor in green, white-veined and red Turquino marble, while the stucco-lined walls are decorated with delicate gilded arabesques evoking the bucolic pleasures of country life.

QUEEN OF THE STAGE

Gardening and the theater—the two great pleasures of the period—were brought together by Marie Antoinette at the Trianon. In 1779, she decided to build a little theater like the one she had known in her Austrian childhood, and as was then the custom in numerous country houses, where hostesses amused themselves by staging little plays for their guests. The following year, Richard Mique built "a little theater" decorated in shades of blue and gold, with a wooden auditorium painted in faux white-veined marble and embellished with sculptures made of carton pierre. Equipped with all the latest stage machinery, it was in many ways a smaller version of the great court theater that was the royal opera house at Versailles.

Marie Antoinette loved to perform on stage. In these private amateur theatricals, she would sing and act the lead parts, playing shepherdesses and servant girls including Colette in *Le Devin de village* ("The Village Soothsayer") by Jean-Jacques Rousseau and Rosina in Beaumarchais's *Le Barbier de Séville*. She was accompanied by the "*troupe des Seigneurs*," made up of her friends and court nobles such as the king's brothers, the Comte d'Artois and the Comte de Provence: "It was royally badly acted," observed Mme Campan. The audience of around a hundred was hand-picked and composed exclusively of the queen's circle, seated in boxes fitted with grilles, with a handful of servants also discreetly watching through the oeil-de-boeuf windows beneath the cornice.

NOCTURNAL EXTRAVAGANZAS

The entertainments that Marie Antoinette organized at the Trianon were spectacular. The first festivities, in honor of her brother Emperor Joseph II on September 3, 1777, consisted of a small fair, with ladies of the court running the various stalls, and the queen herself manning a refreshments stall. The three most dazzling nocturnal extravaganzas were mounted in 1781 for Joseph II's second visit, in 1782 for Grand Duke Paul and Grand Duchess Maria Feodorovna of Russia, and in 1784 for the Swedish king Gustav III. On these occasions, the garden paths were strewn with sand to protect the guests' silk slippers, and every corner of the gardens was lit up with thousands of lamps: lights buried in the ground to illuminate the buildings; floating lanterns concealed in clumps of faux rushes; Chinese lanterns hung from trees; blazing bundles of firewood hidden in ditches; and "magic tableaux" consisting of paper screens up to twenty feet (six meters) tall, oiled to make them transparent, painted with all manner of images including rocks, shrubberies, trees, and flowers, and backlit. With these lavish nocturnal spectacles, Marie Antoinette revived the legendary splendor of the festivities mounted by Louis XIV. In the eyes of the courts of Europe, these extravaganzas—conceived on a scale that remains astounding to this day—represented a consecration of the Trianon and a dazzling manifestation of the personal power of the queen.

PAGE 106 *The* Comtesse d'Artois in court dress, colored print after Claude-Louis Desrais. PAGE 107 The Queen's Little Theater. With its handsome blue-and-gold decorations in carton pierre, this "little paper theater" built by Mique next to the Trianon's garden à la française, was one of the most charming of court theaters. Today it is the only theater in France, and one of only a handful worldwide, where the stage machinery of an eighteenth-century theater may still be seen. Miraculously, the original stage sets have also been preserved. LEFT Claude-Louis Châtelet, *Celebration given by the Queen in the Gardens of the Petit Trianon in 1781.* In the summer of 1781, Marie Antoinette gave a lavish celebration in honor of her brother Emperor Joseph II. Amid this scene of magical splendor, Claude-Louis Châtelet depicted the illuminations of the Rock and the Belvedere, their golden reflections transforming the lake into a sheet of flame.

The "Style Trianon"

In this small country château devoted to the worship of nature, the paneling is of peerless elegance, and the gilding that is so ubiquitous at Versailles is replaced with combinations of white and pastel shades. The famous "Trianon gray," now understood as a warm pale gray, in fact corresponds to a nineteenth-century incarnation of the Trianon paneling. The recent restoration of the building has revealed that the dominant color on the paneling was a green, like the green Campania marble of the floors, that was designed to bring the bucolic atmosphere of the surrounding gardens into the house. Viewed as the embodiment of the queen's indulgence in lavish pleasures and spendthrift extravagance, at the Revolution the Petit Trianon became the focus of wild fantasies, of imaginary excesses such as rooms lined from floor to ceiling with diamonds, or columns studded with sapphires and rubies. In reality, the Trianon represents, in Pierre de Nolhac's elegant description—perfectly capturing a style that affects simplicity while at the same time displaying an ineffable refinement—"pure good taste in place of the expected luxury."

The Trianon also represents an unprecedented degree of harmony between "inside" and "outside," a spirit of place summed up by the remarkable "ears of corn" (*épis*) furniture made by Georges Jacob for the queen's bedchamber. The wooden frames are decorated with carved and painted ears of corn interwoven with tendrils of honeysuckle and jasmine, lilies of the valley, pine cones, and wickerwork motifs; the white bazin fabric, meanwhile, is embroidered with roses, buttercups, and the cornflowers that are such a characteristic feature of the decorative schemes in the Petit Trianon. All these motifs drawn from the meadows and hedgerows are captured with peerless and meticulous verisimilitude.

This in the end is the essence of the *style Trianon*: the use of flowers and floral motifs on every surface and in every form, roses and lilies of the valley, myrtle and lilies, sunflowers and ears of corn, strewn in all their natural simplicity, woven into graceful garlands, arranged in artful bouquets, mingled with motifs of pearls and ribbons, and scattered in profusion over furniture and objets d'art.

FACING PAGE Detail of the armchair of the "ears of corn" (*épis*) set made by Georges Jacob and supplied by the queen's private Garde Meuble in 1787 for her bedchamber at the Petit Trianon. This is a rare example of a chair that has preserved its original upholstery. The woodwork was carved by Jean-Baptiste-Simon Rode and painted by Jean-Baptiste Chaillot de Prusse, while the embroidered fabric was woven by Marie-Olivier Defarges. The "rustic" decorative details are painted "in the colors of truth and nature", and the uprights, intertwined with tendrils of jasmine, are topped with clusters of pine cones.

Queen of Fashion

Marie Antoinette established a new relationship between the monarchy and its age, in which—instead of embodying timeless tradition, age-old and unchanging—she was queen of the here and now. The confidence of her tastes, which always captured the spirit of her time, and her audacious penchant for wearing "avant-garde" creations earned her the status of a fashion icon. All the ladies at court and in the capital copied her style and wanted to look like her. The young queen was not *in* fashion—she *was* fashion.

ROSE BERTIN, FRANCE'S FIRST "GRAND COUTURIER"

In 1770, Rose Bertin, a modest dressmaker from Picardy, had her own dress shop, *Le Grand Mogol*, on rue du Faubourg-Saint-Honoré in Paris. By the time she was presented to the queen, she counted all the ladies of the court and the aristocracy among her clientele. Endowed with a razor-sharp sense of style, boundless creativity, and a shrewd head for business, Bertin enjoyed a meteoric rise through the ranks of society. It was her meeting with Marie Antoinette, however, that was to prove the turning point in her career. Corporation law decreed that, as a "seller of fashions" she could neither sew nor sell gowns herself, but could only accessorize them with "all the little details with which ladies adorn themselves." It was on these "adornments," constantly updated with newer, more fashionable versions, that Marie Antoinette (with the expert guidance of Rose Bertin) was to spend such colossal sums. Frocks and fashion were her obsession, and she was prepared to lavish unlimited effort and expense in order to ensure that each of her appearances was more dazzling than the last. In defiance of court etiquette, she even received Rose Bertin in her private apartments for tête-à-tête consultations. Dubbed the queen's "Minister of Fashion," Bertin made use of her unprecedented access to the court to become the foremost seller of fashions in the kingdom, amassing a vast fortune along the way.

Rose Bertin invented haute couture in the modern sense of the term. In her lifetime she became a celebrity on an extraordinary scale, and her name became a luxury brand. In a field where prices had hitherto been based on the costs of the raw materials and the hours of work involved, she viewed her profession as an art, resting on an element of creativity that was impossible to quantify or cost, which in turn justified her exorbitant prices. She also grasped the essential principle that in order to create a need she had to innovate on a permanent basis, and she was constantly changing her collections and introducing new lines. Finally, she had an instinctive understanding of the importance of publicity, and knew that by choosing a "celebrity" to wear her designs she would become famous throughout Europe. And Marie Antoinette—beautiful, constantly in the public eye and avid for anything new—was her ideal model. On some fashion engravings, indeed, the queen's head was attached to gowns that she had never worn, purely for the sake of generating sales.

PAGE 113 *Marie Antoinette in Court Dress*, by Jean-Michel Moreau the Younger, colored print. FACING PAGE *New robe à la circassienne in Italian gauze lined with Indian taffeta*, engraved by J. Pelicier after Claude Louis Desrais, published in 1780 in the *Galerie des modes et des costumes français*. The *circassienne* was a variation on the polonaise gown, with the skirt of the manteau rounded at the bottom and caught up at the sides. The *Galerie des modes et costumes français*, with engravings after drawings by Claude-Louis Desrais, Pierre Thomas le Clerc, Watteau de Lille, and Augustin de Saint-Aubin, published by Esnault et Rapilly from 1778 to 1787, is considered to be the first French fashion magazine. BELOW *Winter court dress during the reign of Louis XVI, trimmed with marten tails*, by Sébastien-Jacques Leclerc and Etienne Claude Voysard, colored etching. Costume of a court lady worn for the Queen's balls during the reign of Louis XVI, by Claude-Louis Desrais and Nicolas Dupin, colored etching. The fabrics used for formal court dresses varied according to the season: velvets and furs in winter, satins in spring, and taffetas and airy silks and gauzes in summer.

THE QUEEN'S GARDEROBE

Marie Antoinette's wardrobe was overseen by her Garde Robe, one of the five departments of her royal household. The service was run by the *dame d'atours*, or "lady of the royal attire," an important and sought-after position at court, who commanded a staff of chambermaids, wardrobe attendants, seamstresses, laundry maids, and valets. Three times a year, with each new season, thirty-six toilettes were ordered, divided into three groups of twelve: twelve formal court dresses for grand occasions; twelve "rich gowns with wide panniers"; and twelve "little extravagances" for afternoon wear and informal suppers. In addition to these came gowns for specific occasions, such as maternity dresses and riding habits for the hunt.

FACING PAGE Design by Christian Bérard for the Théâtre de la Mode, Paris, 1945. This show, which featured large mannequin dolls dressed by the great Paris couture houses and presented in theatrical settings designed by the most distinguished interior designers of the age, traveled the world to display French preeminence in matters of fashion.
ABOVE Presentation of a Maggy Rouff model from the Fall–Winter 1952 Haute Couture collection in the Council Chamber at Versailles. A sumptuous gown in white satin sewn with sequins and fine braid, with a long stole in azure blue tulle.

FACING PAGE *Angie*, ecru hand-embroidered antique faille dress, Christian Dior Haute Couture collection Fall–Winter 2000–2001.
RIGHT *Marie Antoinette, Queen of France*, in a court gown embellished with pearls, swags, and acorns, with a violet cloak embroidered with gold fleur de lis, colored print engraved by Deny after Claude-Louis Desrais.

COURT GOWNS, OR "ROBES EN CHEMISE"

The image of the queen is generally associated with sumptuous court gowns, with boned stomachers and wide panniers covered with heavy silk brocades woven in Lyons, followed by layer upon layer of fabrics spangled with precious stones and embellished with an infinite array of sequins, fringes, puffs, ruches, embroidered swags, and more. The wearing of formal court dress was a genuine physical ordeal for women, however. From around 1780, accordingly, Marie Antoinette recommended that it should only be worn on rare occasions, and replaced it with the more informal *robe à la française*, or "sack-back" gown, distinguished by its train falling from the neckline in loose box pleats at the back, and its looser and more comfortable waist.

BELOW *Feminine fashions and accessories, including a muff and hats*, color print by A.B. Duhamel after Jean Florent, from *Le magasin des modes nouvelles françaises et anglaises décrites d'une manière claire et precise*, 1789.

FACING PAGE *Robe à la française* or "sack-back" gown, c. 1750–60, satin edged with ribbon, gray and green silk, applications of green silk chenille. Often associated with the great painter Antoine Watteau, the *robe à la française*, here richly embroidered with silk flowers, was distinguished by its train falling from the neckline in loose box pleats at the back and extended by a train. It was worn over a boned stomacher, forming a triangular shape descending to a point; the skirt was broadened at the hips by panniers; and the facings of the pagoda sleeves ended at the elbows and were embellished with two scalloped flounces.

For afternoon wear, and for her excursions to the Petit Trianon, Marie Antoinette preferred the gossamer-light gowns that had recently begun to be imported from England. These "chemise" dresses, which became known at the French court as *gaulles* or *chemises à la reine*, were made from a single length of lawn or muslin, which was caught in at the waist with broad ribbon sashes tied in bows at the back, like little girls' dresses. Generally they were worn with hair tumbling loose to the shoulders, and accessorized with broad-brimmed straw hats trimmed with flowers and feathers. This new freedom in dress was symbolic of a more general change for women, with new and modern ideas of simplicity and freedom that also represented a break with the traditional pomp and pageantry of the monarchy. And it was also a sign of a yearning for the bucolic lifestyle advocated by Rousseau and other major figures of the Enlightenment.

Copied by fashionable ladies throughout Paris, these simple chemise dresses made Marie Antoinette look dangerously like an actress, doing away with the age-old distinction between the queen and her subjects as symbolized in the sumptuous opulence of the royal wardrobe. On August 25, 1783, at the Salon of the Académie Royale at the Louvre, Élisabeth Vigée Le Brun unveiled a new portrait of Marie Antoinette, in which the queen's appearance was simple and natural, unadorned by jewels and wearing a fashionable white *chemise à la reine*, with her hair worn loose under large straw hat. The portrait caused a scandal: the dress was too simple, too intimate, and the public went away with the impression that the queen was wearing her negligee. The queen was supposed to be remote and beyond reach, yet here she seemed to be offering herself to the hungry gaze of her subjects. Deemed indecent, the portrait was promptly withdrawn from the Salon, and Élisabeth Vigée Le Brun hurriedly painted another one, *Marie Antoinette with a Rose*; put on display before the end of the exhibition, this subsequently became one of the most universally recognized portraits of the queen.

FACING PAGE *T*he famous portrait of *Marie Antoinette with a Rose* now hangs in the Petit Trianon at Versailles. Following the public scandal caused by her portrait of *Marie Antoinette in a Chemise Dress* at the Salon of 1783 (p.104), Élisabeth Vigée Le Brun replaced it with this new portrait of the queen holding a rose. She kept the same pose, but depicted the queen in more conventional fashion, corseted in a glossy blue satin sack-back gown trimmed with fine lace, with a striped ribbon bow at her bosom, two rows of pearls at her throat, and three on each wrist.

"The dressing of the princess was a triumph of etiquette. Every detail was laid down. The lady-in-waiting and the lady of the royal attire—together if both were present—aided by the first lady of the bedchamber and two ladies in ordinary, would carry out the principal service; but there were distinctions between them. The lady of the royal attire would pass the petticoat and present the gown. The lady-in-waiting would pour the water for the washing of the princess's hands and pass the chemise. When a princess of the royal family was present at the ceremony, the lady-in-waiting would yield this last function to her, but she would not cede it directly to princesses of the blood. Each of these ladies was punctilious in her observance of this ritual, as though it were their right.

One winter's day, it happened that the queen, already completely undressed, was about to put on her chemise; I had unfolded it and was holding it ready; the lady-in-waiting entered, hastily took off her gloves and took the chemise. There was a scratching at the door, and Madame la Duchesse d'Orléans came in; removing her gloves, she came forward to take the chemise, but the lady-in-waiting was not supposed to give it directly to her; so she gave it back to me, and I gave it to the princess. More scratching at the door, and Madame la Comtesse de Provence arrived; the Duchesse d'Orléans gave her the chemise. The queen had her arms folded over her chest and looked cold. Madame saw her painful situation and merely cast away her handkerchief while keeping her gloves on; as she put the chemise over the queen's head she disarranged her hair. The queen laughed to conceal her impatience, but not before saying several times through her teeth, 'How odious! Such importunity!'"

MME CAMPAN, *The Private Life of Marie Antoinette, Queen of France and Navarre*, 1822.

FACING PAGE *E*cru hand-embroidered duchess satin coat, Christian Dior Haute Couture collection Spring–Summer 2005.

NECESSARY ACCESSORIES

Gauze fichus and lace mantelets, garters, bonnets and hats—under the influence of Rose Bertin, accessories became the essential complements, adding the final touch to every elegant lady's outfits. And perhaps the most popular accessory of all was the fan. In the eighteenth century, Paris was the capital of the fan-making industry, and master fan-makers produced an endless variety of creations. The slats might be made of pierced and engraved mother-of-pearl or ivory, inlaid with gold or silver and embellished with sequins, embroidery or feathers, while the folded fan itself was decorated with charming scenes painted in gouache. Although originally designed to cool flushed cheeks in summer, fans became no less de rigueur in winter. An ambassador for French elegance and style, the fan became not only an indispensable attribute of feminine finery, but also an essential weapon in a lady's armory of coquetry and flirtation. Gracefully raised or lowered, fluttered or snapped shut, sometimes equipped with lorgnettes and other ingenious devices, fans could be used to reveal or conceal, to disguise many a discreet confidence or smile, or to hide blushes and heightened emotions.

FACING PAGE *On* a balcony of the Royal Opera at Versailles, Marie-Hélène Arnaud models a Lanvin-Castello design of 1957.
BELOW Fans made in Paris, c. 1776–1800: the fans consist of folded paper embellished with sequins and painted with bucolic scenes of fêtes galantes, while the slats are of pierced and engraved ivory inlaid with gold and silver.

THE QUEEN'S COLOR PALETTE
Marie Antoinette loved pastel shades—tones of green and blue, especially periwinkle blue, lilac and mauve, and also pink, which she stopped using when she was thirty, although she always favored white for the decorations of her apartments. For fabrics she was also very fond of floral motifs on a plain ground, and the highly fashionable "zebra" stripes. Constantly in the public eye, she also inspired new colors, such as the "*cheveux de la reine*" based on the ash blond shade of her hair, and "*puce*," meaning "flea," the name coined by Louis XVI for the brownish purple of one of her gowns, which rapidly gave rise to a bewildering variety of associated shades including *cuisses de puce* (flea's thighs), *dos de puce* (flea's back), *vieille puce* (old puce), *puce effrayée* (frightened flea), and more. This was an age that tended to the dramatic and romantic, in colors such as *soupirs étouffés* (stifled sighs), *plaintes amères* (bitter complaints), *cuisse de nymphe émue* (aroused maiden's thigh), or *ventre de carmélite* (Carmelite nun's belly). Alternatively, they could be inspired directly by a distinctly gritty reality, such as *boue de Paris* (Paris mud), *cendres de Londres* (London ashes), *opera brûlé* (burnt opera house, in the wake of the fire of 1781), or even—after the birth of Louis Joseph—*caca dauphin* (princely poop). ❧

FACING PAGE *Madame la comtesse d'Ossun, Garde-robe des atours de la reine. Gazette pour l'année 1782.* This rare volume, preserved in the Archives Nationales, was put together by Geneviève de Gramont, Comtesse d'Ossun, "lady of the royal attire" to Marie Antoinette. Containing seventy-eight samples of gowns worn by the queen from 1782 to 1784, it was not intended for presentation to the queen at her morning levee, so that she could pick her three outfits for the day with a pin, but was rather a record for the household accounts. The colors of the fabric samples offer an evocative palette of pinks and lilacs, plums and puces, blue-greens and grays, as well as a range of floral patterns and stripes.

ABOVE Maison Fabre, artisan glovemakers for four generations, has created a pair of perfumed gloves directly inspired by a pair worn by Marie Antoinette. These long gloves in silk-lined lambskin, hand-embroidered with motifs inspired by one of the queen's gowns, are perfumed with one of her favorite colognes, *Eau d'Ange*. Maison Fabre uses encapsulated natural talc to ensure that the fragrance will last throughout a season.

Extreme Coiffures

Fashions in the late eighteenth century went from one outrageous extravagance to another. Among the most outlandish was undoubtedly the fad for "poufs," as created by Rose Bertin and the queen's wigmaker Jean-François Autier, known as Léonard.

When she arrived at the French court, Marie Antoinette was enchanted by the fashion there for embellishing ladies' coiffures with a wildly eclectic range of ornaments. Poufs were toppling creations padded out with horsehair, gauze, and false hair, on which an unpredictable range of objects might hang or nestle, including cornucopias, exotic birds, tableaux including gardens, prairies, and theatrical scenes, terrestrial globes and ships in full sail. Finishing touches were added with ribbons and flowers, plaits and rolls of hair, and the entire edifice was topped off with a plume of ostrich feathers. These towering creations, many of them well over a foot (30 cm) tall, were like "fortifications constantly on the verge of collapse," according to the Comte de Vaublanc. To please the queen, the rival hairdresser Beaulard attempted to outdo Léonard with the invention of coiffures that concealed hidden mechanisms: "surprise" chignons from which fresh roses bloomed. Soon current events were being played out on the heads of the most fashionable court ladies, who sported with panache confections inspired by "Independence, or the Triumph of Liberty" (in 1779), or the "Hot-Air Balloon" (in 1778). The following year, Marie Antoinette sported a potato flower in her hair, in tribute to Parmentier's promotion of this new food crop, and following the success of the pioneering use of the technique of inoculation to protect Louis XVI against smallpox, she boasted an improbable "inoculation pouf," featuring an olive tree laden with olives around which coiled a serpent menaced by a club that was entwined with flowers, and a rising sun symbolizing the triumph of science over evil.

In Vienna, meanwhile, the queen's redoubtable mother was horrified. When in 1775 she was informed that her daughter was sporting on her head a vertiginous confection of ribbons and feathers that was no less then 36 inches (87.5cm) high, she cautioned her: "You know that I have always been of the opinion that fashion should be followed with moderation, and never to the point of excess. A pretty young queen, with so many charms, has no need of such follies. On the contrary, simplicity in appearance is more flattering, and is better suited to the rank of queen." But the headstrong Marie Antoinette was not to be deterred. When she sent Empress Maria Theresa a new portrait of herself "in the latest fashion," her mother promptly sent it back with an imperious note: "No, there is some mistake, this is not the portrait of a queen of France; it is the portrait of an actress."

FACING PAGE *Independence, or the Triumph of Liberty,"* colored print, 1779.

FACING PAGE *B*lue satin dress with multicolored hand-embroidery, Christian Dior Haute Couture collection, Fall–Winter 2004, photographed by Patrick Demarchelier.
ABOVE *The Preposterous Head Dress, or, The Featherd Lady*, print published in London by Matthias Darly on 20 March 1776. The "featherd lady" is seated at her dressing table, while her hairdresser balances on a stool behind her. Meanwhile a maidservant brings a basket of fruit and vegetables, some of which has already found its way into her mistress's imposing coiffure.

ABOVE *Bonnet à la Victoire, La Candeur, Le Parterre Galant*, fashionable poufs published in the *Première Suite des Costumes Français pour les Coiffures depuis 1776*, colored etching engraved after Gabriel Jacques de Saint-Aubin. Below left, *Collection de la Parure des Dames*, colored etching engraved by Louis Berthet, Paris, c. 1780.

"Then came the vogue for English carriages; the roof inside was very low, so that taller ladies were forced to kneel down in the carriage to avoid crushing their feathers. I saw one lady who was not only on her knees in the carriage but also had her head out of the window. When a lady who was decked out in this motley fashion danced at a ball, she was forced to be constantly vigilant, to make sure that she dipped her head whenever she passed under a chandelier. The effect was as ungainly as may be imagined."

VINCENT MARIE VIENNOT, COMTE DE VAUBLANC, *Mémoires*, 1857.

Queen of Beauty

Was Marie Antoinette beautiful? While most contemporary descriptions praise the delicate oval of her face, her aquiline nose, the porcelain whiteness of her skin, the brilliance of her complexion, her fair hair "of the rarest blond," and the great beauty of her hands, others took delight in dwelling on her piquant imperfections: her forehead was too high and too domed; her eyes were too small, and their "not quite blue" color was too indeterminate; her chin was too defined; and then there was the "Habsburg lip," the full and projecting lower lip that gave her a slightly disdainful look. All in all, as the Comte d'Hézecques noted in his memoirs, "This princess was hardly what one could call pretty."

FACING PAGE *Portrait of Marie Antoinette*, French eighteenth-century school.

PAGE 138 *Young Lady wearing an Elegant Cap or Pouf called La Victoire*, colored etching engraved by Etienne-Claude Voysard after Claude-Louis Desrais. "This accoutrement, no less aristocratic than it is pleasing to the eye," reads the caption, "marries perfectly with the most costly fabrics and is regarded as the stateliest and most noble dress of the Ladies of France."

PAGE 139 Perfume fountain in Chinese porcelain and gilt bronze belonging to Marie Antoinette. This perfume fountain in turquoise Chinese porcelain of the Kangxi dynasty (1662–1722) plays on the contrast between the luminous depths of the color of the enameled porcelain and the gilding of the bronze mounts made in Paris around 1785.

"GRACE ITSELF"

If Marie Antoinette was not a perfect beauty according to the standards of the time, there was one point on which all contemporary observers agreed: the queen's grace. Her grace was majestic, almost otherworldly: "One felt one was seeing the queen of the world," recorded the Duchesse de Polignac, while Horace Walpole was equally impressed, declaring she was "grace itself when she moves." Her lithe, elegant physique, the perfect lines and balletic movements of her ivory-white arms, and her lofty carriage lent her an incomparably regal air: "no other woman carried her head so well, in such a way as to endow all her movements with grace and nobility," testified Gabriel Sénac de Meilhan. So light and fleet of foot was she that Marie Antoinette appeared to glide through the palace without touching the floor.

FACING PAGE *Young Lady wearing an Elegant Cap or Pouf called La Victoire*, colored etching engraved by Etienne-Claude Voysard after Claude-Louis Desrais. "This accoutrement, no less aristocratic than it is pleasing to the eye," reads the caption, "marries perfectly with the most costly fabrics and is regarded as the stateliest and most noble dress of the Ladies of France."

ABOVE Perfume fountain in Chinese porcelain and gilt bronze belonging to Marie Antoinette. This perfume fountain in turquoise Chinese porcelain of the Kangxi dynasty (1662–1722) plays on the contrast between the luminous depths of the color of the enameled porcelain and the gilding of the bronze mounts made in Paris around 1785.

"She had two ways of walking," recalled her page Alexandre de Tilly, "one firm, quick, and always noble, the other more elastic and swaying, almost caressing I would say, but nevertheless still such as to command respect." The queen addressed everyone with a beguiling consideration and courtesy: "Never was a curtsey swept with such grace," observed Tilly, "she would thus greet ten people at once, directing due attention to each with a look or a tilt of her head." Far from the stiff, formal beauty of earlier queens, Marie Antoinette possessed a beauty that was affecting and sincere: her sincerity could be read in her eyes and their ever-expressive looks, eyes that "could assume any character," according to Tilly, and every feeling: "Benevolence or aversion could be read in her eyes in a more singular fashion than I have ever encountered in anyone else."

"Marie Antoinette was tall, with admirable proportions, well rounded but not too much so. Her arms were superb, her hands small and perfectly shaped and her feet charming. No woman in France walked more beautifully than she, carrying her head so high and with a majesty that made her stand out as sovereign among all the ladies of the court, without detracting from the gentleness and benevolence of her expression. It is very difficult to convey to anyone who has not seen the Queen the manner in which such grace and such nobility were united in her.... But the most striking aspect of her features was the brilliance of her complexion. I have never seen such radiance—and radiance is the word, as her skin was so translucent that it allowed no shadows. Thus I was unable to render its effect as I would have wished: no pigments could capture that freshness, those delicate shades that belonged only to those charming features and that I have never encountered in any other woman."

ÉLISABETH VIGÉE LE BRUN,
Memoirs of Madame Louise-Élisabeth Vigée-Lebrun, 1835–37.

FACING PAGE *Portrait of Marie Antoinette, Queen of France*, studio of Élisabeth Vigée Le Brun, c. 1778.

BEAUTY SECRETS

In the previous century it had been the whiteness of a person's linen that indicated their social status; in the eighteenth century it was the spotlessness of the skin that lay beneath that mattered. As the widespread belief that water was dangerous—spreading disease by dilating the pores—lost its hold, so the "pleasures of bathing" were rediscovered. The private apartments at Versailles boasted bathrooms equipped with running hot water and two baths, one for washing and the other for rinsing.

In parallel, cosmetics reached new heights of refinement, and ladies' dressing tables were now graced with rich *nécessaires* comprising combs in ivory and mother-of-pearl; powder boxes in agate, gold, or enameled silver; face powders; pomades; soaps; beauty spots; and perfumes in rock crystal bottles. Hair was powdered, perfumed, and sometimes colored.

Perfume occupied an essential place in the rituals of beauty. Jean-Louis Fargeon, "master glovemaker and perfumer" to the queen, created floral compositions for Marie Antoinette to match her tastes and moods. In the second half of the eighteenth century, advances in distilling techniques made it possible to produce and mix fragrances of much greater subtlety, so lending a new impetus to the perfume industry and distancing it definitively from the worlds of physicians and apothecaries. Now perfume was no longer therapeutic but cosmetic, and Fargeon elevated it into an art. In his celebrated treatise *L'Art du Parfumeur*, he revealed the full extent of his palette of fragrances, including myrrh, musk, ambergris, aloe, sandalwood, tuberose, bergamot, hyacinth, daffodil, orange blossom, jasmine, lavender, violet, and rose. Perfume was rarely applied to the skin at this period, nor even to clothes: rather it was handkerchiefs, gloves and fans that gave off clouds of fragrance. Marie Antoinette never went out without a pair of gloves scented with jasmine and pink, which would be presented to her on a rich gilt salver, accompanied by her handkerchief, by her lady of the bedchamber.

ABOVE *Nécessaire* casket for perfumes and toiletries in mother of pearl, gold, silver, and gilded silver, Pierre Médard Mothet after Carle Van Loo, 1764–65.
FACING PAGE *Marie Antoinette as Erato*, Ludwig Guttenbrunn, 1788.

"*You* know that I have always been of the opinion that fashion should be followed with moderation, and never to the point of excess. A pretty young queen, with so many charms, has no need of such follies. On the contrary, simplicity in appearance is more flattering, and is better suited to the rank of queen. The queen must set the tone, and everyone will hasten to follow even your little failings. But I, who love and follow my little queen at her every step, feel bound to warn her about this little frivolity."

Letter from **MARIA THERESA** to Marie Antoinette, March 5, 1775.

ABOVE AND FACING PAGE *D*etail of one of the doors of Marie Antoinette's boudoir at Fontainebleau. The panel is painted in white gold framed by yellow gold. At the bottom is a large antique vase spilling over with flowers depicted in their natural beauty, set among graceful tendrils that rise to frame the central figure of a woman at her toilet.

BELOW AND FACING PAGE The paneling in Marie Antoinette's bathroom, situated in her private apartments on the ground floor of the palace, features decorative motifs on a watery theme, with crayfish, swans drinking from a basin, rushes, reeds, dolphins, shells, pearls, and coral, as well as items from a lady's toilette. It is furnished with a *lit à la polonaise*, on which the queen would rest after bathing. The bed, which came from Louis XVI's bathroom at Fontainebleau, is covered with a satin counterpane embroidered with the interlaced monograms of the king and queen.

Affaire du Collier de la Reine.

Représentation exacte du grand Collier en Brillants des S.rs Bœhmer et Bassenge.

Fac-similé d'une gravure du temps appartenant à M. Henry Mesnier, chef du service administratif à l'Imprimerie Nationale.

The Queen's Diamonds

When Marie Antoinette came to France, she brought with her a sumptuous jewelry collection, of which a meticulous inventory—the *État des Diamants de Madame la Dauphine*—was drawn up within a day of her arrival. To this lavish personal collection Louis XV added all the diamonds and pearls of his late daughter-in-law Maria Josepha of Saxony, mother of the future Louis XVI, and it was further swelled by the prodigious quantities of diamonds she received on her marriage. The queen wore these precious stones mounted as jewelry, on aigrettes in her coiffures, and sewn on to ceremonial gowns.

Despite all these riches, Marie Antoinette was recklessly profligate in her spending on herself, squandering vast amounts that became ever more ruinous as the years went by. In 1776, she bought a pair of girandole earrings set with six enormous diamonds, made by the crown jeweler Boehmer. She persuaded Louis XVI to foot the bill of 460,000 livres, a colossal sum that the king arranged to pay from his own purse, obtaining credit over four years. The following year she spent a further 250,000 livres on a bracelet. Far away in Vienna, her mother was growing increasingly alarmed by her outrageous extravagance, which seemed to know no bounds.

It was against this background that the infamous incident that was to become known as the Affair of the Diamond Necklace blew up, with the spectacular arrest in the Hall of Mirrors on August 15, 1785 of Cardinal de Rohan. In this shady affair, the cardinal, who had lost the queen's favor and was prepared to go to any lengths to regain it, was duped by an unscrupulous adventuress, Mme de la Motte, who convinced him that the queen wanted to buy a diamond necklace of breathtaking lavishness, and that she wished him to take charge of the delicate negotiations. The notorious necklace, created by the crown jewelers Boehmer and Bassange, comprised no fewer than 647 diamonds, and at 1,600,000 livres its price was astronomical. Although the queen was wholly innocent in the affair, there was a wealth of circumstantial evidence—the profligate style in which she lived; the unsuitable friendships she fostered; her voracious and well-known appetite for jewels; and the subterfuges to which she had resorted in the past to obtain them without the king's knowledge—to convince everyone privately of her guilt. By the time Marie Antoinette found out that the necklace had been bought in her name it was already too late: the damage was done and her reputation was tarnished beyond repair.

FACING PAGE *Exact depiction of the great diamond necklace made by MM. Boehmer and Bassenge, "showing the diamonds at life size."*

"*All the news from Paris is that you have bought some bracelets at a cost of 250,000 livres, that your finances are in disarray and weighed down with debt, and that to remedy this you have given away diamonds at a very low price, and that people suppose that you draw the King into these pointless extravagances, which for some time now have been mounting up and putting the State in the dire straits in which it now finds itself.*"

Letter from **MARIA THERESA** to Marie Antoinette, September 2, 1776.

FACING PAGE Lace ribbon brooch, Cartier, 1906. In the early twentieth century, when the fashion for Art Nouveau was at its height, Louis Cartier found inspiration in eighteenth-century jewelry albums, such as the *Traité des pierres précieuses et de la manière de les employer en parure* by Jean Henri Prosper Pouget, published in Paris in 1762. Illustrated with large color plates, this album offers models for designs of pure fantasy. Thanks to his pioneering use of platinum, which could be shaped into settings that were highly flexible and almost invisible, Cartier was able to create lacy creations such as this, in which every diamond was revealed in all its éclat.

Queen of Pleasures

The stately rhythms of court life were too slow for Marie Antoinette: she preferred to live in the moment. To quell her boredom and drown her ennui, she threw herself into a whirl of parties and pleasures with all the enthusiasm of youth.

FÊTES AND EXTRAVAGANZAS

Marie Antoinette's childhood at Schönbrunn had left her with a passion for entertainments and making music, dressing up, and playing pranks. At the French court, during the carefree years when she was surrounded by flattering courtiers and frivolous friends, she thought only of amusements: little afternoon recitals in her private apartments, at which she played the harpsichord and the harp and sang "quite prettily"; grand concerts that she laid on in the palace gardens, with her favorite composers Gluck and Grétry; and games, especially billiards and blind man's buff, and gambling, notably at faro or pharaoh, a card game at which she would lose astronomical sums. In summer she loved excursions and escapades with her bosom companions, walks punctuated by refreshments, and hunting parties (on which she rode "like a man," rather than sidesaddle); in winter there were wild sledge races along the snowy paths of the palace gardens or even on the frozen Grand Canal, and snowballing parties at the Petit Trianon.

FACING PAGE *Marie Antoinette in Hunting Attire*, by Joseph Krantzinger, 1771.

ABOVE *Marie Antoinette, Reine de la Pensée*, playing card by Bayard, Paris, 1816.
FACING PAGE *The Game of Whist*, etching by Jean Dambrun after Jean-Michel Moreau the Younger.

"She loved everything that lulled and nurtured reverie, every pleasure that spoke to young women and distracted young queens: private retreats where friendships could blossom, intimate conversations to which her soul could yield, and nature, her friend, and the woods, her confidantes, and the distant horizon where sight and thought were lost to view, and flowers and their eternal celebration."

EDMOND AND JULES GONCOURT, *Histoire de Marie Antoinette*, 1858.

PAGES 156-57 Detail from the layette chest of Marie Antoinette's first son Dauphin Louis Joseph, made at his birth on October 22, 1781.
FACING PAGE *Portrait of Queen Marie Antoinette*, engraving by Antoine Phélippeaux after Jeanne Dabos, published in Paris by Madame Bergny, supplier of prints to HRH the Princesse de Lamballe.

FACING PAGE *Costumes of Marie Antoinette, the Comte and Comtesse de Provence and the Comte d'Artois at a court ball in 1785*, engraved in 1843 by Héliodor Joseph Pian after a drawing by Louis-René Boquet, costume designer for the theater and the opera under Louis XV and Louis XVI.

BELOW *The Masked Ball. Celebrations given for the King and Queen by the City of Paris on 23 January 1782, on the occasion of the birth of the Dauphin, at the Hôtel de Ville*, engraved after Jean-Michel Moreau the Younger.

THE QUEEN'S BALLS

Charged by Louis XVI with organizing the program for the court theater, Marie Antoinette put on two performances a week by the French court theater troupe and one by their Italian counterparts. She also revived the tradition of giving grand formal and masked balls in the Salon d'Hercule, outdoing herself at very appearance with a new costume of unsurpassed extravagance and sophistication. While her own balls at Versailles became famous throughout Europe, she also loved to go to balls at the Paris Opera, sometimes secretly and staying till dawn. Accompanied only by the Comte d'Artois, she was convinced that she went unrecognized in her velvet mask, when in fact everyone present knew who she was from the moment of her arrival, and merely pretended not to out of tact. Marie Antoinette loved to go incognito: when she could shrug off the persona of the queen, she could exist in her own right. These nocturnal jaunts to Paris, unaccompanied by her husband, scandalized her courtiers and left them feeling abandoned. Meanwhile her family in Vienna did not mince their words: "You are getting older and you no longer have the excuse of youth," lectured her brother Emperor Joseph II. In her passion for fêtes and extravaganzas, Marie Antoinette was following in the footsteps of Louis XIV and Louis XV before her. The difference—and it was a significant one—was that now for the first time the "supreme organizer of these pleasures" was a woman.

> "*They say she does not dance in time, but then it is wrong to dance in time.*"
>
> **HORACE WALPOLE**

ABOVE *S*hoe made for Marie Antoinette, collected on August 10, 1792, Paris workshop, white faille and brown ribbon, 1792.
FACING PAGE *Angie*, ecru hand-embroidered antique faille dress, Christian Dior Haute Couture collection Fall–Winter 2000–2001, photographed by Patrick Demarchelier.
PAGE 164–65, BOTTOM *Decorations for a Dining Room in the Wooden Houses for the Queen's Balls in 1785*, Pierre-Adrien Pâris.
PAGE 165, TOP Kirsten Dunst as Marie Antoinette in Sofia Coppola's eponymous film, 2006.

"*She believed that she was never recognized, when in fact she was known by everyone present from the moment she entered the auditorium: pretending not to recognize her, we invariably came up with stratagems to secure her the pleasure of remaining incognito.*"

MME CAMPAN, *The Private Life of Marie Antoinette, Queen of France and Navarre*, 1822.

"*What* is it that you seek in going incognito and playing a role that is not your own? Do you believe, in spite of it all, that people do not recognize you, and that the remarks they make are not in any way intended to be overheard by you, when they are said in order to amuse you and to make you imagine that they are uttered in all innocence, but they have their effect. The very place itself is of extremely ill repute; what do you hope to find there? Honest conversation? Not with your friends, the mask makes this impossible. And dancing too! So why these escapades, this mischief-making, this mixing with crowds of libertines, whores, and foreigners, hearing the things they say and perhaps replying in kind? It is indecent! I must tell you that this is the matter that most scandalizes all those who love you most and who are right-thinking. The king abandoned at Versailles for the entire night, while you mix in such company and are mistaken for the riffraff of Paris! I tremble now for the happiness of your life, for this cannot go on much longer; and unless you prepare yourself for it the revolution will be cruel."

JOSEPH II, *Reflections given to the Queen of France*, 29 May 1777.

FACING PAGE *The Farewells*, engraved after Jean-Michel Moreau the Younger, 1777.
PAGE 168 *Le Jeu du Roi in the Hall of Mirrors on the occasion of the the Dauphin's second marriage to Maria Josepha of Saxony on the night of 9 February 1747*, by Charles-Nicolas Cochin the Younger.
PAGE 169 View down the Grand Perspective from the central window of the Hall of Mirrors.

"*In spite of the pleasures of Carnival I am still faithful to my harp, and am told I am making progress. I also sing at my sister Madame's weekly concerts. Although we are very few at these occasions, we derive great enjoyment from them.*"

Letter from **MARIE ANTOINETTE** to Maria Theresa, January 13, 1773.

ABOVE *The Perfect Chord*, Isidore Stanislas Helman after Jean-Michel Moreau the Younger.
FACING PAGE This harp by Jean-Henri Naderman, "master luthier in ordinary to Madame la Dauphine," reputed to have belonged to Marie Antoinette and now displayed in her private Grand Cabinet, is richly decorated with a flower garland twined around the column. The queen would study the harp—that most Rousseau-esque of instruments—with her master for an hour and a half or two hours every morning, and in the afternoon she would play what she had learned. Marie Antoinette had only to take up the harp for this instrument, though still at this time slightly rudimentary and outlandish, to become fashionable.

FACING PAGE *I*n this painting from around 1783, Louis Auguste Brun, called Brun de Versoix, depicts the queen engaged in one of her favorite pastimes, the hunt. Instead of riding sidesaddle, as ladies were supposed to do, Marie Antoinette preferred to ride like a man, sitting astride her mount. Her mother tried in vain to dissuade her from this most unseemly practice, which was to be strenuously discouraged if she wanted to bear children.

ABOVE, TOP The gardens at Versailles under snow. ABOVE, BOTTOM *Lady on a sledge*, 1729.

The Queen's Inner Circle

"Kings lack for nothing but the pleasures of a private life: their sole consolation for this great loss may be the charms of friendship and the loyalty of their friends." Marie Antoinette seems to have adopted this famous adage of La Bruyère as her own: imprisoned in an unsatisfactory marriage, she sought refuge in friendship. Court etiquette decreed that the French queen had a ready-made circle of friends in her ladies-in-waiting. But Marie Antoinette did not intend to have her friends chosen for her. She lost no time, moreover, in putting a distance between herself and the chilly and protocol-obsessed Comtesse de Noailles, openly poking fun at her by dubbing her "Madame l'Etiquette." Turning the established order—hitherto set in stone—on its head yet again, she let it be known that she would herself choose her "bosom friends": feelings and qualities of character clearly mattered more to her than the protocols of rank and precedence.

So it was that Marie Antoinette surrounded herself with a select circle of elegant and amusing gentlemen of her own age, who formed a little court within the court, an inner coterie or *"élixir de cour"* of whom everyone else was jealous. The Comte d'Artois, Marie Antoinette's dashing and flamboyant brother-in-law, was the leading light of this group of gallant young blades, who also included the Duc de Coigny, Baron de Benseval, Comte Esterhazy, the Duc de Guines, the Comte de Vandreuil, and "the handsome Lauzun," a prolific seducer with a stormy love life who fancied the queen was in love with him. Their favored pastimes were gambling and nocturnal escapades and outings, and they were devoted aficionados of everything "modern" in all its forms.

FACING PAGE *Charles-Philippe de France, Comte d'Artois (future King Charles X) in formal robes of the Order of the Holy Spirit,* by Antoine-François Callet, 1779.

ABOVE *Portrait of Mme Élisabeth*, Élisabeth Vigée Le Brun, 1782, Château de Versailles
Mme Élisabeth, Louis XVI's youngest sister, was eighteen when this portrait was painted in 1782.
With her voluptuous figure and large and expressive brown eyes, the young princess
is depicted *en belle jardinière*. She holds a posy of freshly picked wildflowers,
and wears a straw hat with more meadow flowers and ears of corn pinned to its broad brim.
The bucolic atmosphere captures the pastoral pleasures relished by the queen and her sister-in-law
at the Petit Trianon, where Madame Élisabeth had her own apartments.
FACING PAGE *Portrait of the Princesse de Lamballe*, studio of Antoine François Callet, 1778.
The Princesse de Lamballe was Marie Antoinette's first great friend at the French court before
being supplanted in the queen's affections by Mme de Polignac. In this magnificent portrait,
a symphony in gray, she appears in the full flush of her youthful beauty.

As for her female favorites, no sooner had Marie Antoinette arrived at Versailles than she formed an intense friendship with the Princesse de Lamballe, a virtuous widow of just eighteen, with extremely pretty looks but naïve in character and not over-endowed with sparkle or wit. When Marie Antoinette became queen, she included the princess in all her pleasures and reintroduced the position of superintendent of her household for her. But then she dropped her for a new and livelier friendship with the Comtesse de Polignac, a young woman of grace, cheerfulness, spirit, and piquant wit.

They met at a ball at Versailles in the fall of 1775. When Marie Antoinette asked why she had not noticed her before, the countess confessed that she lacked the means to keep up appearances at court. Surprised and touched by this candor, the queen was determined to rectify the injustice of her new friend's fate at all costs. She proceeded to shower her and her "clan" with favors and privileges, to secure her "the finest lodgings at Versailles," to make her a duchess, to appoint her as governess of the royal children, and to bestow upon her daughter Aglaé the immense sum of 800,000 livres. But despite all the scandal that ensued, the friendship was a deep one that was to endure until Marie Antoinette's death. The queen was also very fond of her sister-in-law Madame Élisabeth, Louis XVI's youngest sister, ten years younger than him and intelligent, modest, virtuous, and—as the events of the Revolution were to show—capable of heroic courage.

FACING PAGE *I*n this handsome portrait painted by Élisabeth Vigée Le Brun in 1782, the year in which she was appointed governess to the royal children, the Duchesse de Polignac wears a gauzily light chemise gown, tied in a bow at the back with a wide buttercup-yellow sash. Her broad-brimmed straw hat, with a posy of wild flowers tucked carelessly in its ribbon band and a black follette ("scatterbrain") ostrich feather, is also in the very latest fashion.

Queen of Hearts

The favor enjoyed by the queen's inner circle gave rise to resentment in certain quarters. The closeness of some of her friendships also prompted rumors of excessive intimacy. While this gossip was unfounded, there was nevertheless one man who stirred her deepest feelings.

A HANDSOME SWEDISH OFFICER

Born in the same year as Marie Antoinette, Count Hans Axel von Fersen was the elder son of one of the wealthiest and most powerful men in Sweden. In 1774, at the end of his Grand Tour of Europe, he arrived at the court of France, where he made a great impression: "Of all the Swedes who have been here in my time," wrote the Swedish ambassador, Count von Creutz, "he has been granted the warmest reception in the highest circles. He has been treated most favorably by the royal family. He has conducted himself with a wisdom and decorum that would be impossible to emulate. Possessed of the finest figure and intelligence, he could hardly fail to succeed in society, and did so in complete fashion." The young man was "handsome as an angel," according to the Comtesse de Boigne, and had "a burning soul beneath an icy exterior," in the words of one of his friends, Madame de Korff. Tall and slim with intense dark eyes, in his uniform of the Swedish royal dragoon guards (reputed to be one of the most elegant in Europe), he cut an irresistibly dashing figure. This handsome newcomer had all the court ladies in a swoon.

FACING PAGE *Portrait of Axel von Fersen*, Carl Frederik von Breda, c. 1800. "I must confide in Your Majesty," wrote the Swedish ambassador to his king, Gustav III, "that the young Count von Fersen has been looked upon with such favor by the queen that this has caused offence to a number of people. I confess that I cannot help thinking that she harbored a tendresse for him: I have seen signs that are too clear to leave any doubt."

COUP DE FOUDRE

It was on January 30, 1774, at a masked Carnival ball at the Paris Opera, that Marie Antoinette first encountered Count von Fersen. Initially he did not recognize her in her mask, but after dancing together they both felt an immediate bond. During the course of the evening, Fersen afterward wrote in his diary, the queen conversed with him "at length." They parted at dawn, and soon the young officer returned to Sweden. When Fersen was officially presented to her at court on August 25, 1778, four and a half years later, Marie Antoinette exclaimed, "Ah! An old acquaintance!" She had not forgotten him. Over the winter of 1779, she made him part of her inner circle. But the affection she showed him, innocent though it was, inflamed jealousies in others. In the circumstances, Fersen decided the best course of action was to go off to fight in the American War of Independence: "By taking himself far away," reflected Count von Creutz, "he also left behind all the dangers. But naturally it required a degree of resolve beyond his years to overcome such charms."

He was away for another four years. On his return in 1783, Marie Antoinette used her influence to obtain him a French regiment, the Royal Swedish. They grew close again, but more discreetly: Fersen no longer appeared at official receptions, and he pursued other romantic interests.

"THE MOST BELOVED AND THE MOST LOVING OF MEN"

Numerous contemporary accounts leave little doubt as to the reality of these tender feelings. Mme Campan was a privileged witness, and Count von Creutz observed Marie Antoinette's emotional state when Fersen left for America: "In the final days the queen could not take her eyes off him: and as she gazed at him, they would fill with tears." Their letters also betray the depth of their feelings, with Marie Antoinette describing Fersen as "the most beloved and the most loving of men." Writing to his sister on July 31, 1783, Fersen confessed, "I have decided never to marry.... Since I cannot belong to the only person to whom I would like to belong, the only who truly loves me, I prefer to belong to no one." He wanted to do his utmost to safeguard the queen's reputation, which was being dragged ever lower with each passing day. In craving the company of a man who was not her husband, who was not even French moreover, she had seriously compromised herself. To dissemble her attachment and cover her tracks, she therefore decided to admit other Swedish gentlemen into her inner circle, such as Count von Stedingk, who suddenly found himself invited to suppers in the king's private apartments, a privilege that was above his rank. Instantly, the jealousy that had been directed at Fersen was now transferred to the hapless Stedingk.

RIGHT *Young Officer in a Zebra Coat*, from *La Galerie des modes et costumes Français, dessinés d'après nature*, 1778–87.

FACING PAGE Gentleman's richly embroidered coat and waistcoat, worn by Axel von Fersen, France, 1785.

"*I exist my beloved and it is in order to adore you. I have been so worried about you, and I so pity you for all that you suffer in lacking all news of us. Heaven will grant that this reaches you. Do not write to me, it would expose us, and above all do not return here on any pretext. They know that it was thanks to you that we escaped from here; if you were to appear, all would be lost. We are held under guard day and night; it is all the same to me. You are not here. Do not fear, nothing will happen to me. The Assembly wants to treat us kindly. Farewell, most beloved of men. Calm your anxieties if you are able. Look after yourself for my sake. I may no longer be able to write to you, but nothing in the world can prevent me from adoring you until I die.*"

Letter from **MARIE ANTOINETTE** to Count von Fersen, June 29, 1791.

FACING PAGE *Marie Antoinette of Austria, Queen of France and Navarre*, by Jean-Joseph Bernard, 1780.

AN UNCONSUMMATED LOVE?

While there can be no doubt about the couple's feelings for each other, the question remains: was their love ever consummated? Modern historians are far more preoccupied with this question than contemporary opinion was, since at court keeping up appearances counted for quite as much as the actual facts of the matter. Stefan Zweig wrote eloquently of Fersen's last visit to the queen in her prison at the Tuileries, on the night of February 13, 1792: "It is certain that even if Fersen had not become Marie Antoinette's lover long before, he must have become so on that last fateful night, which he had obtained at the cost of the most incomparable display of human courage." In 1950, this theory was corroborated by tests carried out at the state technical institute in Stockholm. Infra-red photography revealed what lay underneath a crossed-out passage in Fersen's diary: on that same night in February, after noting that he had "not seen the king," he added that he had "stayed there," before scoring out this admission. Marie Antoinette and Fersen therefore spent the night alone with each other.

Most historians in France today tend to believe that the relationship was platonic, and that Marie Antoinette and Fersen remained chaste lovers, or *"amants restreints,"* in the phrase of the historian Pierre Audiat. Other historians suggest that, having decided to have no more children, and no more relations with her husband, the queen might have allowed herself this "weakness": since there was no longer any question of childbearing there would be no question of the crime of *"lèse dynastie,"* or betrayal of the dynasty. Historically there is no evidence to support this view. But the censoring of some passages in Fersen's letters by his descendants, the destruction of his correspondence with the queen, and the disappearance of his diary entries for the crucial years from 1776 to 1791 have all encouraged such speculation, in the way that mysteries and enigmas will always lend credence to myths.

What remains so remarkable about this story is Fersen's absolute loyalty to Marie Antoinette, a devotion that was as sincere as it was limitless, with all the appearance of a love that would forever remain unconsummated. Amid the tumult of the Revolution, when all her friends had fled, Fersen was the only one who was there for her. Obsessed with the need to save the queen, he made diplomatic representations to seek aid from foreign sovereigns, and he attempted to rescue her from incarceration in the Tuileries by helping to organize the flight to Varenne on June 21, 1791. But it was all in vain. A few months before her death, Marie Antoinette sent him one final message, bearing her seal with Fersen's arms; written in Italian, it said, "*Tutto a te mi guida*," "All things lead me to you." ❧

FACING PAGE *M*iniature portrait of Axel von Fersen, painted in gouache by Gabriel Jean Joseph Hubert Le Monnier after Carl Frederik von Breda.

"The sole object of my interest no longer exists, in her alone everything was united for me, and only now do I realize how truly attached to her I was. I cannot stop thinking about her, her image follows me and will follow me everywhere and always, I want only to speak of her and to recall the best moments of my life, alas all that remains to me of her is her memory, but I shall keep it and it will leave me only with my death. I have given orders to buy everything that may be found of Elle in Paris, everything that I have of her is sacred for me, they are relics that will be the perpetual object of my constant admiration."

Letter from **COUNT VON FERSEN** to Sophie Piper, November 17, 1793.

RIGHT *Portrait of Marie Antoinette*, attributed to François Hubert Drouais and reputed to have been given by the queen to her confessor in 1781.

"*Elle*"

In both his diary and his letters to his sister and confidante Sophie Piper, Fersen was always careful to shield the queen's identity. Initially he referred to Marie Antoinette by the code name "Josephine," later replacing this simple with "*Elle*." "I must warn you, dear Axel," his sister wrote to him, "for the love of *Elle*, to whom this news would cause mortal suffering were it to reach her. You are observed and discussed by all. Think of unhappy *Elle*. Spare her this grief, of all griefs the most mortal."

Immured in the Tuileries after the failure of the flight to Varenne, the queen was closely guarded. Her only means of communicating with Fersen was through a secret exchange of letters. From June 1791 to August 1792, when she was transferred to the Temple Prison, they wrote to each other using a code that they had worked out between them. Some of these letters were published by Fersen's great-nephew in 1877, with some passages mysteriously deleted and indicated by ellipses. These "redacted" sections proved to match the passages written in code. Two French cryptographers have recently carried out an analysis of four autograph letters from Marie Antoinette that entered the collections of the Archives Nationales in 1982, rare survivors of the campaign of destruction waged by Fersen's descendants. In 2014, they succeeded in deciphering the code, and were able to reveal the passages that had remained secret ever since they were first read: "I exist my beloved and it is in order to adore you"; "Farewell. Pity me. Love me. Above all, judge me in all that you will see me do only after hearing me. If the creature whom I adore and whom I shall never cease to adore were to disapprove of me for an instant I should die"; "Farewell, the most beloved and the most loving of men. I embrace you with all my heart"; "I shall love you unto death." Marie Antoinette's feelings were here revealed with a new and fervent power.

FACING PAGE *T*opiary vases in the Bosquet de l'Encelade in the gardens at Versailles.

ABOVE *Letter* from Marie Antoinette to Axel von Fersen, dated July 8, 1791. This letter in Marie Antoinette's hand contains letters coded by the queen, with the keyword since repeated ad infinitum below. The code used by Marie Antoinette and Fersen was highly sophisticated. The method they chose was the polyalphabetic system, with each letter of the alphabet corresponding to a pair of letters, and a keyword that changed with each message. The processes involved in writing and deciphering the code were long and laborious, as the queen complained to Fersen in a letter dated November 2, 1791.

FACING PAGE *Portrait of Marie Antoinette*, Wilhelm Böttner, 1784.

Queen and Mother

One day in the summer of 1778, Marie Antoinette advanced on Louis XVI, her expression gravely indignant: "Sire, I come to protest to you about one of your subjects, who makes so bold as to kick me in the stomach." Thus, in her own original and playful way, she informed the king that he was to be a father. On December 19 she gave birth to her first child. In motherhood she found a fulfillment that was to curb the frivolous and futile excesses of the life she had led hitherto.

FACING PAGE *The dauphin Louis Joseph Xavier of France taking Communion in the chapel of Meudon*, by an unknown artist, late eighteenth century.

ROYAL BIRTHS

"The queen is in labor!" No sooner had this pronouncement been uttered by the *accoucheur* Vermond, charged with delivering the royal infant, than streams of curious onlookers rushed into the queen's bedchamber and crowded against the balustrade. As she suffered the first pangs of labor, ministers, ambassadors, members of the royal family, and servants all flocked to watch. The birth of the Children of France always took place according to a scrupulously observed protocol, in the presence of a throng of courtiers, in order to avert any possibility of substitution of the royal infant. Marie Antoinette's labor was thus a particularly grueling experience, with unruly spectators clambering on to the furniture and hanging from the curtains in order to get a better view. The heat was suffocating, and Marie Antoinette was desperate for air. In the end, although it was in the depths of winter, Louis XVI commanded that a window should be flung open. When the queen gave birth, at half past eleven in the morning, she understood from a discreet sign given to her by the Princesse de Lamballe that the baby was a girl. The child was given the name Marie-Thérèse. The courtiers clapped and cheered, before returning to their usual routine while discussing the best moments of the "performance."

FACING PAGE *Maternal Pleasures*, by Isidore Stanislas Helman after Jean-Michel Moreau the Younger.

Since the baby was a girl, it was imperative that the queen should become pregnant again without delay, a subject on which her mother lectured her relentlessly: "All that you tell me about your daughter has given me great pleasure," wrote Maria Theresa on April 1, 1780, "and I share all your mother's feelings in the doings of this dear little creature. It is all so very touching! But we need a Dauphin. I am seized with impatience, my age scarcely permitting me to wait." Within two months she had returned to the subject: "We need a Dauphin. I have been discreet hitherto, but at length I shall become importunate. It would be fatal not to provide more children for this dynasty, for they say that your dear daughter is a marvel of health and charm."

Early the following year, the queen's second pregnancy was announced. This time, when the first pangs came on October 22, 1781, Marie Antoinette was careful to conceal them in order to steal a march on the organizers of the ceremonial ritual that would follow. With a mere dozen spectators present, her labor was easier to bear than on the previous occasion. The long-awaited dauphin, named Louis Joseph, was passed to the appropriately named Madame Poitrine (Madame Bosom) for nursing. On March 27, 1785, the queen gave birth to a second son, Louis-Charles, Duc de Normandie.

A MODEL OF MATERNAL AFFECTION

Although the French royal children were traditionally looked after by a governess, with the boys "joining the men" at the age of seven, Marie Antoinette wanted to share in her children's early years, and even planned to feed her own daughter—something that was unthinkable for a queen of France. Overwhelmed by the strength of her maternal feelings, she watched her children growing up with ever-growing tenderness and love. Giving free rein to her affection, she loved to play games such as blind man's buff with them, under the disapproving gaze of the ladies of the court. She gave her daughter, who grew into a rather cool, imperious child, the pet names "Mousseline" and "Madame Sérieuse," while the little Louis-Charles was her "Chou d'amour," or "darling cream puff." The dauphin Louis Joseph, meanwhile, suffered from delicate health. Tuberculosis of the spine meant that he was forced to wear a steel corset and to get about the palace in a wheelchair. But his intelligence, his sweet nature, and the courage he displayed in the face of his illness compelled the admiration of all.

FACING PAGE *Marie Antoinette, Queen of France, with her two Eldest Children*, by Eugène Bataille after Adolf Ulrik Wertmüller, 1867. Madame Royale and the dauphin Louis Joseph walking in front of the Temple of Love in the gardens of the Petit Trianon in 1785.

A THOROUGHLY MODERN EDUCATION

The king and queen personally oversaw the education of their children. In his way, Louis XVI was a modern father, who was attentive to his children's development and taught them geometry, geography, and astronomy. In 1786, he gave the dauphin a remarkable terrestrial globe endowed with an elaborate mechanism by Merklein, "showing the depth of the seas and the celestial firmament." Marie Antoinette taught the children to read, and introduced them to the fables of La Fontaine, as well as the writings of Rousseau, Voltaire, La Rochefoucauld, and Montesquieu. She also introduced them to the simple virtues of rural life in her Hamlet, where they would help Mme Richard feed the goats and sheep, and vied with each other for rides in the little cart drawn by a white billy goat. To imbue them with a sense of values, she found a little girl from a humble background—Ernestine Lambriquet, the daughter of one of her chambermaids—as a playmate for Marie-Thérèse, and to teach them about generosity, she showed them toys and then explained to them that she was going to use the money she would have spent on them in order to give alms to the poor.

Marie Antoinette applied the modern principles of child-rearing that had been popularized by Jean-Jacques Rousseau in *Emile, or On Education*. "The children were always encouraged to have complete trust in me," wrote their governess Mme de Tourzel, "and when they had done something wrong to tell me so themselves. This meant that in scolding them I appeared upset and sorry rather than cross about what they had done. I instilled it in them that when I said yes or no there would be no argument, but I always gave them a reason appropriate for their age, so that they would not think that it was mere whim on my part." Being parents also brought the royal couple closer together, forging family bonds that were to come to the fore at the Revolution. The closeness of Louis XVI and Marie Antoinette with their children, quite unlike any previous French monarch, was symbolic of an era that set new store by the value of childhood, and promoted the values of a harmonious family life.

LEFT *Marie Antoinette's Two Oldest Children*, Élisabeth Vigée Le Brun, 1784. This charming portrait of the queen's two oldest children hung in the bedchamber of her private apartments at Versailles. Contrary to the royal tradition of putting little boys in breeches, the little dauphin wears a sailor suit in the English fashion, with ankle-length silk satin trousers.

FACING PAGE *Portrait of the Dauphin Louis-Charles, future Louis XVII*, by Jacques-Fabien Gautier d'Agoty, c. 1789.

A MOTHER'S GRIEF

In 1786, when she was pregnant once again, Marie Antoinette commissioned Élisabeth Vigée Le Brun to paint a large portrait of her surrounded by her children. By presenting herself as the mother of the future king, simply dressed and in the most human of poses, she hoped to restore her increasingly tarnished reputation. Severely damaged by the affair of the diamond necklace, accused of plunging the royal purse into deeper debt and denounced for keeping scandalous company, she was the target of pamphleteers who spread increasingly virulent rumors, even to the point of casting doubt on the legitimacy of the royal children. Seated in the center of the composition, the queen appears majestic and serene. Louis Charles, still a baby, wriggles on her lap, while Madame Royale affectionately holds her mother's right arm and leans her cheek against her shoulder. The dauphin Louis Joseph stands on his mother's left, pointing to an empty cradle that might belong to Louis Charles. But the sad truth is that this is a reference to little Sophie Béatrice, who was born on July 9, 1786 and died before her first birthday. Élisabeth Vigée Le Brun had started work on the portrait a little before Sophie's death, and had intended to place the sleeping baby, so young she was not yet weaned, in the cradle. She had already made a preparatory sketch of the sleeping infant. In the finished painting, the cradle remains tragically empty. When the painting was put on display at the Salon, viewers were struck by the queen's mournful expression, and by the blank, empty look in her eyes. At court, there was general astonishment that she could feel such grief "for a baby." At Versailles, the painting was hung in the Salon de Mars.

On June 4, 1789, when the Estates General were in full session, the dauphin Louis Joseph died. When the grief-stricken king heard that the representatives of the Estates General were impatient for his presence, he cried out, "Are there no fathers among them?" After the death of the dauphin, Marie Antoinette could no longer bear to look at this scene of a happiness that had vanished forever. The painting was taken down and put in store: turned to the wall, it was to remain forgotten until the early twentieth century.

LEFT *The queen at her toilette*, the frontispiece of a book by the hairdresser Depain, Paris, 1780.
FACING PAGE *Marie Antoinette and her Children*, Élisabeth Vigée Le Brun, commissioned in 1786 and completed for the Salon of 1787. It took two years for Élisabeth Vigée Le Brun to complete this monumental portrait. In choosing to wear little jewelry, and none at her throat, the queen seemed to be saying that her children were her only treasure. She hoped thus to regain the affection of a public who would be well acquainted with the episode from ancient Roman history in which the virtuous Cornelia Africana, mother of the Gracchi, was asked why she did not adorn herself with the jewels that befitted her status. In reply, she pointed to her sons, saying, "These are my jewels."

"Chou d'Amour"

After the death of the dauphin, Marie Antoinette heaped her affections on Louis Charles. Robust in health and bursting with her life, he was her complete happiness. He was also possessed of a lively intelligence and a great generosity of feeling for his age, and it is hardly surprising that her pet name for him was the tenderly affectionate "*Chou d'amour*." On the morning of January 1, 1790, for example, when he was four years old and the royal family was being held in captivity, he came to his mother in triumph, declaring: "Here is your New Year's present, Maman: I have kept my promise, and now I can read!" The Duchesse de Tourzel, governess to the royal children after the departure of Mme de Polignac in 1789, reported the description that Marie Antoinette gave her of her son, which in its perceptiveness and understanding of a child's psychology remains touching to this day:

"My son is aged four years and four months less two days; I shall not speak of his height nor of his outward looks, you have only to look at him; his health has always been good, but when he was still in his cradle we noticed that his nerves were very delicate and that the slightest noise affected him…. The delicacy of his nerves is such that he is always frightened by unfamiliar noises; he is frightened of dogs, for example, if he hears them barking close by. I have never forced him to see them, because I believe that as his reason develops his fears will pass; like all robust, healthy children, he is very scatterbrained, very thoughtless and has temper tantrums, but he is good-natured, very affectionate and even tender, when his scatterbrained nature permits; he has an inordinate pride in himself, which if well directed may one day prove to be to his advantage; until he feels at ease with someone, he can control himself and even swallow his impatience and quick temper to appear gentle and kind; he is very loyal when he has promised something, but he is also very indiscreet, and will easily repeat what he has heard, and sometimes without wishing to tell an untruth he will add what he has seen in his imagination, this is his greatest fault, and one for which he must be firmly corrected; for the rest, I repeat, he is good-natured, and with sensitivity combined with firmness, though without being too severe, it will be possible to make him as we wish him to be, but he has a great deal of character for his age, and severity would make him rebellious; to give an example of this, even when he was tiny the word "sorry" offended him; when he is in the wrong he will do and say anything we might wish, but only with tears and endless complaining will he say he is sorry."

FACING PAGE Louis Pierre Deseine's terracotta bust of Louis Charles, Duc de Normandie and future Louis XVII, sculpted in 1890, stands on a carved and gilt walnut console table with an Italian griotte marble top, made by the Rousseau brothers in 1781 for the Cabinet de la Méridienne. In the center of the waist is a large carved medallion depicting a radiant dolphin surrounded by flaming hearts, an allusion to the long-awaited birth of the first dauphin, Louis-Joseph.

Queen of the Meadows

A bucolic, idealized notion of rural life became all the rage in the late eighteenth century. Marie Antoinette's response to this vogue for pastoral romanticism was the building of her Hamlet, a model village at the far northern edge of the Trianon gardens. In 1783 she visited several other similar follies, including the one at Chantilly, and commissioned the architect Richard Mique to draw up plans. She was personally involved at every stage of the project, from sketch and models to corrections and adjustments. In 1787, she could at last take her guests there for arcadian outings. Sentimental though it was, this "comic opera version of a country village," as the Goncourt brothers described it, made strenuous attempts to appear authentic, even down to the artificial patina of age with which the buildings were veneered to make them look even more picturesque—so creating what became known as the "decrepit style."

FACING PAGE *View of the Hameau of Marie Antoinette*, taken from *Versailles, Paris and Saint Denis*, published in London in 1809, colored print after a watercolor by John Claude Nattes.

THE QUEEN'S DOMAIN

The Hamlet consisted of eleven cottages dotted around an artificial lake, five of which were reserved for the use of the queen and her guests. The Queen's House was the largest, and the only one to boast two storeys and a tiled roof. It consisted of two buildings linked by a wooden pergola, which was decorated with white ceramic flower pots from Saint-Clément, bearing the queen's monogram in blue. This floral display was described by the Comte d'Hézecques as "a veritable hanging garden." On the ground floor were a dining room and a games room, while the first floor housed large and small salons and a chinoiserie gaming room. On the other side were a billiard room downstairs, and a small apartment upstairs, reached by a spiral staircase. Behind the picturesquely rustic façade, the rooms were sumptuously appointed.

To the right of the Queen's House lay the Boudoir, the smallest building in the Hamlet. With a marble fireplace, a mirror, and a parquet floor, this was where the queen could entertain one or two guests in complete privacy. Behind the house was the Rechauffoir, or warming kitchen, for reheating dishes that had been brought over from the palace kitchens. It contained a bread oven, a water tank, a fireplace with roasting spit, and a press containing the table linen and silverware. Further off stood the Watermill, which was never used to mill grain but was instead a laundry. Devoid of any mill machinery, it boasted only a decorative waterwheel that the little stream flowing from the lake would never have had the force to turn.

"*Nearby lay the real farm, where the queen had a magnificent herd of Swiss cattle that grazed the surrounding fields.*"

COMTE D'HÉZÈCQUES, *Recollections of a Page at the Court of Louis XVI*, 1873.

FACING PAGE The Sampling Dairy (*Laiterie de Propreté*) in the Queen's Hamlet at Trianon. The white marble tables would be covered with dairy products laid out in exquisite porcelain services for Marie Antoinette and her guests to enjoy. BELOW Detail of a gilt bronze ram's head on the fountain.

ABOVE Design by Jean-Jacques Lagrenée le Jeune for the "gobelet cornet," or cone-shaped goblet, of the porcelain service for the dairy at Rambouillet. Of the four different designs for milk cups, this was the only one without a saucer, and was designed to fit inside a bowl. The shape is derived from antique vases, while the upswept handles recall the outlines of the kantharos, or Etruscan drinking vessel. The base, handles and rim all bear antique-style geometric designs in black on an orange background, while in the center a cow suckles her calf beneath a frieze of vines.
FACING PAGE This remarkable breast-shaped, flesh-colored bowl was supplied in 1788 for Marie Antoinette's dairy at the château of Rambouillet by the royal porcelain factory at Sèvres.

THE COTTAGES

The river formed a sort of natural boundary between the decorative part of the Hamlet and the working buildings. "Real" agricultural workers and their families were housed in the cottages, and were required to tend their smallholdings and harvest produce for the queen. M. Bréval, head gardener at the Hamlet, was responsible for the picturesque kitchen gardens attached to the cottages, and for their crops of firm round cabbages, cauliflowers, French beans, peas, and artichokes.

Opposite the Billiard Room, the Dovecote housed pigeons, with an enclosed poultry yard behind. Vestiges of the original Barn and Working Dairy (*Laiterie de Préparation*) can still be seen. The Dairy housed a stone table surrounded by console tables laden with tin utensils. An adjoining room contained a stove and fireplace for pasteurizing the milk. The finished dairy products were then placed in an icebox, a small insulated cabinet cooled by blocks of ice that were delivered daily.

To the south, opposite the Watermill, lay the Sampling Dairy (*Laiterie de Propreté*), where the queen and her guests would taste the produce of the farm. Thanks to the popularity of works such as Rousseau's *Julie, or the New Héloise*, milk was considered as an ideal food that fostered a state of physical and moral purity. Inside, the furniture was of white marble, and a little rivulet trickled across the floor to cool the summer air. Console tables were laden with exquisite porcelain bowls containing fresh cheeses, ice creams, fromage blanc, and strawberries and cream, one of Marie Antoinette's favorite desserts. Attached to the Dairy was the Hamlet's tallest building, the Marlborough Tower. Standing like a lighthouse beside the lake, this served as the point of departure for boating trips or carp-fishing parties. With its impressively curving external staircase leading up to a panoramic terrace embellished with pots of hyacinths, stocks, and geraniums, this was one of the prettiest of all the follies in the Queen's Hamlet.

FACING PAGE *View* of the Marlborough Tower from the loggia of the Queen's House in the Queen's Hamlet at the Petit Trianon. Standing like a lighthouse on the shores of the Great Lake, the tower served as the point of departure for boat trips and carp-fishing parties.

THE ROYAL FARM

The Farm lies a little way out of the village to the east, and was originally endowed with small apple and cherry orchards. With its hens, sheep, goats, cows, pigs, and rabbits, it was a proper working smallholding, a miniature farm that also supplied the palace kitchens. The cows—including Brunette, Marie Antoinette's favorite—and the bull were imported from the high alpine pastures that had become so fashionable since Goethe and Rousseau had sung the praises of lofty mountain landscapes. The original billy goat, proving immune to the charms of the nanny goats, was replaced by another animal, which the queen insisted must be white and good-natured, imported from Freiburg. The farmer, Valy Bussard, kept careful accounts for this little model farm and submitted them every quarter.

LEFT *The* entrance porch to Marie Antoinette's farm in the Queen's Hamlet at the Petit Trianon. The farm, which lay outside the village, was home to a variety of livestock including a bull, cows, and calves brought from Switzerland, sheep, nanny goats and a "docile white billy goat."

"*In the houses I imagined rural feastings, in the meadows wanton games, along the river, baths, walks, and fish, on the trees delicious fruit, under their shade voluptuous meetings, on the mountains tubs of milk and cream, a charming laziness, peace, simplicity, and the pleasure of going one don't know where.*"

JEAN-JACQUES ROUSSEAU, *The Confessions*, volume II, 1767.

PAGES 216–17 *The Queen's Hamlet at the Petit Trianon*, watercolor by Claude-Louis Chatelet from *Vues et plans du Petit Trianon à Versailles*, 1786.
FACING PAGE The Marlborough Tower and the Sampling Dairy in the Queen's Hamlet at the Petit Trianon. The tower served as a boathouse for the Hamlet's boat, and as a store for tackle for fishing for pike and carp. The panoramic viewpoint at the top of its great curving stair was used as a signaling post for communicating with the palace. The tower's name, reflecting the anglomania then in vogue, was a reference to a song composed on the death of Louis XIV's old adversary the Duke of Marlborough in 1722.

The Final Act

In the end, throughout the twenty years of her reign, all that Marie Antoinette saw of her kingdom was the enchanting decors of her palaces. The woman who so loved to play act had lived out her life on the stages of Schönbrunn, Versailles, Trianon, Marly, Fontainebleau, Saint-Cloud, and Rambouillet. Until 1789, these were the limits of her world, with the reality beyond remaining hazily out of focus.

Insulated in her Hamlet, in her own little play world of rural life—her perfect pastiche of a country village with its skillfully aged timbers and painted-on cracks, nestling amid carefully tended wildflower meadows—Marie Antoinette was hardly in a position to grasp the significance of the social revolution that was being brought about by the men and women of the Enlightenment. Surrounded by her bosom friends and court ladies, she remained blind to the suffering that surrounded her, and deaf to the rumbles of discontent that were advancing on Versailles.

When reality finally arrived, it was to shatter the idyll of the Petit Trianon. Marie Antoinette was in her mossy grotto, on October 5, 1789, when a page came to hand her a note telling her that six thousand women of the people were marching on Versailles. The queen rushed to join Louis XVI in the palace. She could not then have known it, but she was never to return. Never again would she see her domain. The curtain had fallen. With her departure, Versailles was extinguished.

FACING PAGE *T*his moving pastel portrait by Alexandre Kucharski of Marie Antoinette, which the queen wanted to give to Madame de Tourzel, governess to the royal children, remains unfinished. Working in pastel enabled Kucharski, who succeeded Élisabeth Vigée Le Brun after she was sent into exile in October 1789, to capture the queen's features rapidly, in just one or two sittings. Work on the portrait started at the Palais des Tuileries during the royal family's incarceration there, but was interrupted by the flight to Varennes in June 1791. Kucharski returned to it in 1792, but abandoned it definitively after the incursion into the Tuileries by the people of Paris on August 10, 1792.

Photographic Credits

t: top, b: bottom, l: left, c: center

1: ©Château de Versailles (dist. RMN-Grand Palais)/Christophe Fouin; 2: ©RMN-Grand Palais (Château de Versailles)/Gérard Blot; 4–5: ©RMN-Grand Palais (Château de Versailles)/Gérard Blot; 6: ©Château de Versailles (dist. RMN-Grand Palais)/Christophe Fouin; 7: ©Musée Carnavalet/Roger-Viollet; 9: ©RMN-Grand Palais (Château de Versailles)/Gérard Blot; 10: ©Francis Hammond; 11: ©Östergötlands museum, Löfstad slott; 13: ©Archive Photos/stringer; 14: ©Rue des Archives/BCA; 15: ©Francis Hammond; 16–17: ©Carole Bethuel. *Farewell, My Queen*, based on the novel by Chantal Thomas (éditions du Seuil). With Léa Seydoux, Diane Kruger, Virginie Ledoyen, Xavier Beauvois, Noemie Lvovsky, Michel Robin, Julie-Marie Parmentier, Lolita Chammah, Marthe Caufman, Vladimir Consigny. A movie by Benoît Jacquot. Produced by: Jean-Pierre Guerin, Kristina Larsen and Pedro Uriol. Screenplay: Gilles Taurand and Benoît Jacquot. A coproduction GMT Productions, Les Films du Lendemain, Morena Films, France 3 Cinéma, Euro Media France, Invest Image. A French-Spanish coproduction. With the participation of Canal+, Ciné +, France Télévisions. In association with La Banque Postale Image 5, Palatine Etoile 9, Soficinéma 7. With the support of La Région Ile-de-France in partnership with the CNC, La Procirep, L'Angoa et l'ICAA. Distribution France: Ad Vitam. International Sales: Elle Driver. Soundtrack composed and orchestrated by Bruno Coulais; 19: ©Kevin Mazur Archive/WireImage; 21: ©Schloss Schonbrunn, Vienna, Austria/Bridgeman Images; 22–23: AE/II/2908 ©Archives Nationales (France); 25: ©Kunsthistorisches Museum, Vienna, Austria/Bridgeman Images; 27: ©Hofburg, Vienna, Austria/Bridgeman Images; 28: ©Château de Versailles (dist. RMN-Grand Palais)/Jean-Marc Manaï; 29: ©RMN-Grand Palais (Château de Versailles)/Gérard Blot; 30: ©Château de Versailles (dist. RMN-Grand Palais)/Thomas Garnier; 32 and 33: ©Francis Hammond; 34: ©RMN-Grand Palais/Agence Bulloz; 35: ©RMN-Grand Palais (Château de Versailles)/Gérard Blot; 36–37: ©BPK, Berlin (dist. RMN-Grand Palais)/image BPK; 38–39: ©BnF; 41: ©RMN-Grand Palais (Château de Versailles)/Gérard Blot; 42–43: ©Albertina, Vienna; 44–45: ©Château de Versailles (dist. RMN-Grand Palais)/Christophe Fouin; 47: ©Schloss Schonbrunn, Vienna, Austria/Bridgeman Images; 49: ©RMN-Grand Palais (Château de Versailles)/Gérard Blot; 51: ©Francis Hammond; 52, 53 and 54: ©Château de Versailles (dist. RMN-Grand Palais)/Christophe Fouin; 56: ©Francis Hammond; 57: ©Château de Versailles (dist. RMN-Grand Palais)/Christophe Fouin; 58–59: ©Château de Versailles (dist. RMN-Grand Palais)/Thomas Garnier; 60: ©Francis Hammond; 61: ©Château de Versailles (dist. RMN-Grand Palais)/Christophe Fouin; 62 and 63: ©Francis Hammond; 64: ©The Wallace Collection, Londres, Dist. ©The Wallace Collection/The Trustees of the Wallace Collection; 65, 66, 67 and 68: ©Francis Hammond; 69: ©RMN-Grand Palais (Château de Versailles)/Christian Jean/Jean Schormans; 70 and 71: ©Eric Sander; 73: ©RMN-Grand Palais (Château de Versailles)/Gérard Blot; 74 and 75: ©Eric Sander; 76: ©BnF; 77 and 78–79: ©Francis Hammond; 80: ©RMN-Grand Palais (Château de Fontainebleau)/Gérard Blot; 81: ©Eric Sander; 82–83: ©RMN-Grand Palais (musée du Louvre)/Jean-Gilles Berizzi; 84: ©Château de Versailles (dist. RMN-Grand Palais)/Christophe Fouin; 85: ©RMN-Grand Palais (Château de Fontainebleau)/Martine Beck-Coppola; ©Château de Versailles (dist. RMN-Grand Palais)/Christophe Fouin, ©RMN-Grand Palais (musée du Louvre)/Jean-Gilles Berizzi, ©Musée du Louvre (dist. RMN-Grand Palais)/Martine Beck-Coppola; 86, 87, 89, 90, 91, 93 and 94: ©Francis Hammond; 96–97: ©Château de Versailles (dist. RMN-Grand Palais)/Christophe Fouin; 100: ©BnF; 101: ©akg-images; 103: ©akg-images/CDA/Guillot; 104: ©National Gallery of Art, Washington; 105: ©Francis Hammond; 106: ©Château de Versailles (dist. RMN-Grand Palais)/DR; 106–7: ©Château de Versailles, Dist. RMN-Grand Palais/Jean-Marc Manaï; 108–9: ©RMN-Grand Palais (Château de Versailles)/Daniel Arnaudet; 110: ©Francis Hammond; 113: ©Musée Carnavalet/Roger-Viollet; 114: ©RMN-Grand Palais (musée du Louvre)/Madeleine Coursaget; 115l: ©RMN-Grand Palais (Château de Versailles)/Gérard Blot; 116: ©Château de Versailles (dist. RMN-Grand Palais)/DR; 116: ©Adagp, Paris 2015; 117: ©Les Editions Jalou «L'Art et la Mode, 1952»; 118: ©Photo Guy Marineau; 119: ©RMN-Grand Palais (Château de Versailles)/Gérard Blot; 120: ©BnF (dist. RMN-Grand Palais)/image BnF; 121: ©Eric Emo/Galliera/Roger-Viollet; 122: ©BPK, Berlin (dist. RMN-Grand Palais)/image BPK; 123: ©Francis Hammond; 125: ©Laziz Hamani; 126: ©Condé Nast Archive/Corbis; 127: ©Château de Versailles (dist. RMN-Grand Palais)/Christophe Fouin; 128: AE/I/6/2 ©Archives Nationales (France); 129: ©Maison Fabre; 131: ©RMN-Grand Palais (Château de Blérancourt)/Gérard Blot; 132: ©Patrick Demarchelier; 133: ©Courtesy of The Lewis Walpole Library, Yale University; 134tl, tr and br: ©RMN-Grand Palais (Château de Blérancourt)/Franck Raux; 134bl: ©Bibliothèque des Arts décoratifs, Paris, Collection Maciet; 135: ©RMN-Grand Palais (Château de Blérancourt)/Gérard Blot; 137: ©Musée Antoine Lecuyer, Saint-Quentin, France/Bridgeman Images; 138: ©RMN-Grand Palais (Château de Blérancourt)/Gérard Blot; 139: ©RMN-Grand Palais (musée du Louvre)/Martine Beck-Coppola; 141: ©RMN-Grand Palais (Château de Versailles)/Gérard Blot; 142: ©Fr. Cochennec and C. Rabourdin/Musée Cognacq-Jay/Roger-Viollet; 143: ©Archives Alinari, Florence (dist. RMN-Grand Palais)/Marino Ierman; 144 and 145: ©Eric Sander; 146 and 147: ©Francis Hammond; 148: ©RMN-Grand Palais (Château de Versailles)/All rights reserved; 151: Photo N. Welsh, Collection Cartier ©Cartier; 152: ©KHM-Museumsverband; 154: ©RMN-Grand Palais (MuCEM)/Franck Raux; 155: ©RMN-Grand Palais (musée du Louvre)/Thierry Le Mage; 156–57: ©Château de Versailles (dist. RMN-Grand Palais)/Christophe Fouin; 159: ©Musée Carnavalet/Roger-Viollet; 160: ©123RF/Antonio Abrignani; 161: ©BnF; 162: ©Musée Carnavalet/Roger-Viollet; 163: ©Patrick Demarchelier; 164–65: ©Bibliothèque municipale de Besançon, Pâris Vol. 484, n°12; 165: ©Rue des Archives/BCA; 166: ©RMN-Grand Palais (musée du Louvre)/Thierry Le Mage; 168: ©RMN-Grand Palais (Château de Versailles)/DR; 169: ©Château de Versailles (dist. RMN-Grand Palais)/DR; 170: ©RMN-Grand Palais (musée du Louvre)/Thierry Le Mage; 171: ©Francis Hammond; 172: ©RMN-Grand Palais (Château de Versailles)/DR; 173t: ©Francis Hammond; 173b: ©Musée du Louvre, (dist. RMN-Grand Palais)/Marc Jeanneteau; 174: ©RMN-Grand Palais (Château de Versailles)/DR; 176: ©RMN-Grand Palais (Château de Versailles)/Gérard Blot; 180: ©Château de Versailles (dist. RMN-Grand Palais)/Daniel Arnaudet; 179: ©RMN-Grand Palais (Château de Fontainebleau)/Gérard Blot; 180: ©Östergötlands museum, Löfstad slott; 182: ©Galliera/Roger-Viollet; 183: ©Photo Mats Landin ©Nordiska Museet; 185: ©Musée Carnavalet/Roger-Viollet; 186: ©Photo Nationalmuseum, Stockholm; 188–89: ©Josse/Leemage; 190: ©Francis Hammond; 191: 440AP/1 ©Archives Nationales (France); 193: ©BPK, Berlin (dist. RMN-Grand Palais)/image MHK; 195: ©Private Collection/Lylho/Leemage; 196: ©RMN-Grand Palais (musée du Louvre)/Thierry Le Mage; 197: ©RMN-Grand Palais (Château de Fontainebleau)/Gérard Blot; 199: ©RMN-Grand Palais (Château de Versailles)/Gérard Blot; 200: ©Château de Versailles (dist. RMN-Grand Palais)/Christophe Fouin; 201: ©Private Collection/Photo Rafael Valls Gallery, London, UK/Bridgeman Images; 202: ©BnF; 203: ©Château de Versailles (dist. RMN-Grand Palais)/Christophe Fouin; 204: ©Francis Hammond; 207: ©Bibliothèque Historique de la Ville de Paris, Paris, France/Archives Charmet/Bridgeman Images; 208 and 209: ©Francis Hammond; 210: ©Sèvres, Cité de la céramique, Dist. RMN-Grand Palais/Le Studio Numérique; 211: ©RMN-Grand Palais (Sèvres, Cité de la céramique)/Martine Beck-Coppola; 213: ©Château de Versailles (dist. RMN-Grand Palais)/Christophe Fouin; 214: ©Bibliothèque des Arts décoratifs, Collection Maciet, Paris; 214–15: ©Francis Hammond; 216–17: ©De Agostini Picture Library/A. Dagli Orti/Bridgeman Images; 219: ©Francis Hammond; 221: ©Château de Versailles (dist. RMN-Grand Palais)/Jean-Marc Manaï; 223: ©BnF.

List of Works

All works are preserved at the Musée National des Châteaux de Versailles et de Trianon with the exception of those on pages: 11: Östergötlands museum, Löfstad Castle, Linköping; 21: Schönbrunn Palace, Vienna; 22–23: Archives Nationales, Paris; 25: Kunsthistorisches Museum, Vienna; 27: Hofburg Palace, Vienna; 35: Bibliothèque des Arts Décoratifs, Paris; 36–37: Kunstbibliothek, Berlin; 38–39: Bibliothèque Nationale de France, Paris; 42–43: Albertina Museum, Vienna; 47: Schönbrunn Palace, Vienna; 64: Wallace Collection, London; 69: Private collection; 76: Bibliothèque nationale de France, Paris; 80: Château de Fontainebleau, Fontainebleau; 100: Bibliothèque Nationale de France, Paris; 101: Private collection; 103: Biblioteca Estense Univesitaria, Modena; 104: National Gallery of Art, Washington; 113: Musée Carnavalet, Paris; 114: Musée du Louvre, Paris; 116: Private collection; 120: Bibliothèque Nationale de France, Paris; 121: Palais Galliera, musée de la Mode de la Ville de Paris; 131: Franco-American Museum of the Château de Blérancourt, Blérancourt; 133: Yale University Library, New Haven; 134 (top and bottom right): Franco-American Museum of the Château de Blérancourt, Blérancourt; 134 (bottom left): Bibliothèque des Arts Décoratifs, Paris; 137: Musée Antoine Lecuyer, Saint-Quentin; 138: Franco-American Museum of the Château de Blérancourt, Blérancourt; 143: Alinari Archives, Florence; 152: Schönbrunn Palace, Vienna; 154: Musée des Civilisations de l'Europe et de la Méditerranée, Marseille; 155: Musée du Louvre, Paris; 159: Musée Carnavalet, Paris; 161: Bibliothèque Nationale de France, Paris; 162: Musée Carnavalet, Paris; 164–65: Bibliothèque municipale de Besançon; 166 et 170: Musée du Louvre, Paris; 180: Östergötlands Museum, Löfstad Castle, Linköping; 182: Palais Galliera, musée de la Mode de la Ville de Paris; 183: Nordiska Museum, Stockholm; 185: Musée Carnavalet, Paris; 186: National Museum, Stockholm; 189: Private collection; 193: Museumslandschaft Hessen Kassel, Kassel; 195: Private collection; 196: Musée du Louvre, Paris; 201: Private collection; 207: Bibliothèque Historique de la Ville de Paris; 210: Cité de la Céramique, Sèvres; 216–217: Biblioteca Estense Univesitaria, Modena; 223: Musée Carnavalet, Paris.

EXECUTIVE DIRECTOR
Suzanne Tise-Isoré
Style & Design Collection

EDITORIAL COORDINATION
Sarah Rozelle

EDITORIAL ASSISTANCE
Inès Ferrand

GRAPHIC DESIGN
Bernard Lagacé
Assisted by Jean-Rémi Agin

TRANSLATED FROM THE FRENCH BY
Barbara Mellor

COPYEDITING
Helen Woodhall

PROOFREADING
Michael Thomas

PRODUCTION
Barbara Jaegy

COLOR SEPARATION
Les Artisans du Regard, Paris

PRINTED BY
C&C Offset Printing, China

With the participation of the Public Establishment of the Château, Museum, and National Estate of Versailles
Jean-Vincent Bacquart,
Head of the Publishing Department
Marie Leimbacher, Publishing Manager

Simultaneously published in French as
Un jour avec Marie-Antoinette
© Flammarion S.A., Paris, 2015

English-language edition
© Flammarion S.A., Paris, 2015

All rights reserved. No part of this publication may be reproduced in any form or by any means, electronic, photocopy, information retrieval system, or otherwise, without written permission from Éditions Flammarion.

Éditions Flammarion
82 Rue Saint-Lazare
75009 Paris
France
editions.flammarion.com
@styleanddesignflammarion
@flammarioninternational

Legal Deposit: 10/2015
24 25 26 6 5 4
ISBN: 978-2-08-020210-9

PAGE 223 *Marie Antoinette's Hot-Air Balloon*, second experiment carried out in the Cour des Ministres at Versailles by Mr Pilâtre de Rozier, June 23, 1784, colored etching published in Paris by Vachez, 1784.
FRONT COVER *Design for the bolster, headboard, and foot of the queen's bed in the State Bedchamber at Versailles*, workshop of Marie-Olivier Desfarge (detail), gouache, 1786.